Marriage round the clock
(52 ways to stay happily married
even tho' your husband's retired)

MARRIAGE ROUND THE CLOCK

*52 ways to stay happily married
even tho' your husband's retired*

Phoebe Hichens & Joe Wilkerson
Illustrations by Pat Drennan

QUILLER PRESS

First published by Quiller Press Ltd
46 Lillie Road
London SW6 1TN

ISBN 1 870948 26 2

Produced by Hugh Tempest-Radford Book Producers
Printed in Great Britain by Camelot Press plc

The 52 Ways

1. Togetherness – Are you ever alone?   page 13
2. Morning – The importance of the critical '10'.   17
3. Repeating Stories – Still amusing after 20 tellings?   20
4. Physical Affection – And it doesn't have to be SEX.   23
5. Meal Habits – Do you eat with a newspaper, TV, or a person?   30
6. Over and Above the Call of Duty – And the outstanding awards.   33
7. Who's Boss? – Difference between being boss and being bossy.   37
8. Is your Spouse an 'Eccentric'? – Or just unconventional.   40
9. Projects – And their importance.   43
10. Getting Things Done – How to win the war with Parkinson's Law.   47
11. Ingrained Habits – Good, bad, or habitual?   50
12. Marital Encouragement – Don't let it retire when you retire.   53
13. Teasing – With affection – or with a needle?   55
14. Jealousy and Envy – The reasons change, but do they?   58
15. Bones of Contention – A write-out is better than a shoot-out.   61
16. Marital Deafness – Your marriage doesn't suffer from it?   63
17. Holidays – Do you ever take one? Alone?   66
18. Cheerfulness – Where do you fit on a scale of 1 to 10?   69
19. Looking Back – Interesting? Necessary? Or self-indulgent?   72
20. House Rules – Do any of these apply in your house?   75
21. Criticism – A pat on the back, before a kick in the pants.   78
22. Behaviour in Public – And its importance.   80
23. Talk, Talk, Talk, Talk, Talk – Are you listening?   85

24. Your Metabolism – Why do we get fatter as we get older?   92

25. The Booster Programme – Part 1. Foods for your metabolism.   95

26. The Booster Programme – Part 2. Exercise and metabolism.   99

27. The Modern Disease – Allergies.   104

28. Enthusiasm – A great asset.   106

29. Children – Their role in our lives.   109

30. No-Go Areas – The mystery of the locked door.   111

31. Quarrels – And do men sulk more than women?   115

32. Quirks – Do we get quirkier as we get older?   121

33. Pets – Do you have something in common with the Queen?   125

34. Sleeping – Does the time ever come for separate rooms?   128

35. Correcting – 'No dear, it was 1963.'   131

36. Divorce – After forty years?   134

37. Grandchildren – Blessings – or otherwise?   137

38. Memory – Worried about your memory? Forget it.   140

39. Drink – Why women make better alcoholics than men.   144

40. Optimism – Another great asset.   147

41. Laughter – Sorry, but this is a sad subject.   150

42. Friends – Is it back to childhood again?   153

43. Role Reversal – When a husband retires and the wife doesn't. 157

44. Space – And we don't mean outer space.   160

45. Living Habits – Are you an 'average' retired couple?   163

46. Boredom – Is it a factor in retirement marriages?   166

47. Money – When should you start to spend some of your capital? 169

48. Sports – Do you indulge in sport? 50% of you do.   173

49. The Telephone – What's the answer to the answering problem? 177

50. Letters – Can they help your retirement marriage?   180

51. Courtesy – Do you stand up when your wife enters the room?   184

52. A Party Game – One that might help a marriage. Really?   187

A FINAL PS – From both Phoebe and Joe – and a request.   190

Let's get acquainted

Normally you read about the author of a book on the back cover. But this cannot give you much of an idea of them as people.

So, we are going to go against tradition.

Marriage in retirement is an intimate and personal subject; and we have done our best to make this an intimate and personal book. We hope you will look on us not as just authors and researchers, but as friends who have had many of the same retirement experiences as you have. We'd like to tell you a little about ourselves because you cannot be friends with someone you do not know.

First, a few facts. Phoebe Hichens and Joe Wilkerson are both happily married – though not to each other. Both have lived through ten years of marriage in retirement. If you notice a mixture of English-ness and American-ness that's not surprising because Phoebe is English and Joe is American.

Joe retired in 1968 as Executive VP of a major international advertising agency, but subsequently became President of a chain of US radio stations, and Vice-Chairman of a world-wide public relations company. Now he is 100% retired.

He lives on a farm in England, raises cattle and sheep, travels extensively, and is something of a 20th Century freak in that he corresponds prolifically with friends around the world. (Topic 50 tells how letter writing can help a retirement marriage.).

As for Phoebe, in 1952 an advertising executive called Ted Pearce looked out of his elegant London office and said, 'Good

God, what's THAT?' 'THAT' was Phoebe arriving on an ancient bicycle in Wellingtons on her first day as a copywriter in Ted's organization.

Phoebe and Ted were later married – but fifteen years later.

However, Phoebe – who admits to coming from a long line of English eccentrics – surprised her family, and herself, by making a fine salary both in England and New York and was even featured in *The Times*, still not elegantly dressed, as one of the top women in advertising.

After marrying Ted, she wrote features for magazines like *Cosmopolitan*, *Woman's Own*, and *Good Housekeeping*. Mostly on health, slimming, and sex. She also published eight books on subjects as far apart as home made wine and the Royal Family.

Phoebe says of Joe, 'He was for some years my Managing Director. A big, dynamic American with a genius for getting things done. Don't tell him anything is impossible, because he will prove you wrong. No use getting mad at him either, as he can always make you laugh when you were feeling maddest.

'We argued then and we argue now. (You'll notice this in the book.) But I remind him of his comment, 'When two people agree, one of them isn't needed.' And I love the way he gets you to play ping-pong with thoughts, words, ideas – it makes for livelier writing.'

And Joe says of Phoebe, 'She's six feet tall, wonderfully flamboyant, delightfully demonstrative. She enjoys talking, but has the knack of listening. People tell her things that do not come out of run-of-the-mill conversations and interviews.

'Yes, we argue. Some of her opinions strike me as outrageous. But we agree on two things. First, that a book like this needs the man's AND the woman's approach. Second, that humour is a vital ingredient. We enjoy the same stories on retirement marriages which raises a smile or a laugh, as well as making helpful sense.'

Finally, we've truly enjoyed the two years putting this book together. Perhaps that's the greatest compliment co-authors can pay one another.

Phoebe Hichens
Joe Wilkerson

Introduction

To love when you're young
Is easy – and fun.
To love and be old
Is a pot of pure gold.

WHEN we talked with couples when the husband had not yet retired, the prospect of marriage problems hardly figured in their comments. Many were quite starry-eyed about 'Marriage Round the Clock'; and nearly all felt that after so many years together – hiccups and all – they weren't about to come apart at this late stage.

Many marital troubles are, of course, safely in the past. Crying babies, post-natal depression, interfering mothers-in-law, slim-legged secretaries . . . these can usually be forgotten. But a whole crop of new problems are waiting around the corner; and couples who have actually sampled marriage in retirement admit to finding them both unexpected and difficult.

We – Phoebe Hichens and Joe Wilkerson – can begin with personal experience. Both of us have survived many years of retirement marriage (though not, incidently, with each other). But we knew that our experiences were only a beginning. It was essential to spread a wide net and ask complete strangers, as well as innumerable friends and acquaintances, to fill in detailed and intimate questionnaires. We could only hope that they would be willing to cooperate.

They WERE.

The responses were wonderfully uninhibited. Many of our correspondents wrote back more of a book than just the filled-in questionnaire; and often it was sparkling, frank, unpredictable, and funny. Yes, FUNNY. This convinced us that humour should play a part in our finished work, even though the overall goal of 'Marriage Round the Clock' is to offer serious and constructive advice to the retired husband and wife. If something enjoyable, like laughter, can help – why not make the most of it?

And another message came through our research. The viewpoint of men and women can be very different, and this confirmed our feeling that a book like ours needs two authors – one male, one female – so that the approach can be genuinely balanced.

We have written the 52 topics jointly; but occasionally you will find us close to disagreeing. But, after long discussions, we have always been able to find suggestions or recommendations that we both believe in.

You will also find with some topics a personal PS from Phoebe or from Joe where we feel that the man's or woman's viewpoint needs extra emphasis. We also have our favourite stories, drawn from the research, which one or the other of us think will brighten a particular topic.

And talking of topics, you may be wondering 'Why 52?'

Keeping a retirement marriage on the tracks is indeed a 'Round the Clock' occupation. But for those who do not feel like tackling a whole year at a time, how about just one topic a week?

We'll begin with the most crucial topic of all. Can you guess what it is?

With thanks

THIS book has many hundred authors.

But the names of only two appear on the cover. All the others are the retired men and women who opened their hearts and their lives to us.

And the very first thing we want to do is to thank them for being so forthright with us. Without you there would have been no book.

We also are greatly indebted to Rosie Oxley who masterminded the design; to Pat Drennan who did the delightful illustrations; to Hope Chennals who edited the original copy; and particularly to Jeremy Greenwood our patient publisher who had to deal not only with one demanding author, but two.

Finally, we are most indebted to a machine – our Amstrad Word Processor; because unlike most books where an author sits down and writes the text, this book 'developed'. After each interview, after each answered questionnaire, words were changed, or added, or subtracted – new thoughts were introduced. And we typed every word ourselves – many dozens of times.

So we would like to offer Mr Alan Sugar, founder of Amstrad, and his associates, our grateful thanks. Without his magic machine we would have had a hopeless task.

Phoebe Hichens
Joe Wilkerson

Notes

OUR contributors have been remarkably frank with us about their private lives. (Often very private.) For this reason most all of them asked to remain anonymous. We have, of course, respected their wishes. When we make direct quotes from our research we use Christian names plus an initial. Further, in order to maintain complete anonymity we have often changed a name completely. We are sure our readers will understand.

When we finished 'Marriage Round the Clock' we searched for a leading expert on life in retirement to read the book with as critical eye as possible and to give us his comments.

The person unanimously recommended to us was Mr Robert Rose, the Chairman of the recently founded ASSOCIATION OF RETIRED PERSONS.

We were, of course, absolutely delighted to hear Mr Rose's very enthusiastic review (see cover). We greatly appreciate it.

The Association of Retired Persons has been created to serve the very special interests of men and women over 50 planning retirement, or retired. The organization is doing everything possible to make life as exciting and pleasurable as possible for its members.

If you would like to learn more about this interesting Association we suggest you write them. Their address is ARP, Borough Woods House, Shillingford, Bampton, Devon EX16 9BL. We think it will add a new dimension to your life in retirement.

Phoebe Hichens
Joe Wilkerson

1
Togetherness

All day, every day, together
Makes for marital foul weather.

Sam Harris

Iᴛ has been estimated that a working man and his wife spend
about eleven waking hours in each other's company from
Monday morning to Friday evening. When the husband retires it
is likely they will spend fifty-five hours together over the same
period. Five times as long. Any couple, however devoted, will
notice the difference. Any couple, however devoted, may find it
difficult.

Here is one of our favourite stories – and absolutely true –
which illustrates a retirement drama. We'll call it:

THE CASE OF THE WIFE WHO NEVER USED BAD
LANGUAGE

Sheila F. was, by her own admission, rather prim. During 37
years of marriage she and her husband, Max, seldom quarrelled;
and when they did she never dreamed of using bad language. It
wasn't her style.

A few months after Max retired Sheila saw a close friend and
the friend was flabbergasted to hear her say, 'I just might have to
get a divorce.'

A divorce! This long-married, happily-married couple. Why?

The answer had to do with Sheila's Tuesday afternoons. They
had been established in her life as something special. Nothing
elaborate, just the private indulgence of cooking a favourite
lunch and then curling up on the sofa with a good book.

She told us, 'I explained this to Max and he agreed to keep out of my way on Tuesday afternoons. But then one Tuesday it was raining and his golf game fell through. Several other times he wasn't feeling well and had to stay home. Yet another time he just forgot and invited some friends in for lunch.

But last Tuesday, Sheila told her friend, it looked definite. Max was to be off all day meeting his solicitor, and would not be back until evening. Further, it was a rainy, miserable day – ideal for reading in front of the fire.

Togetherness

At noon she went shopping for her cherished lunch. She picked up a book that she had been looking forward to reading. Then she came home. But as she turned into their driveway – there was Max's car. At which she heard herself saying out loud, 'OH SHIT.'

Sheila's query to her friend was, 'Should you stay married to a man whose mere presence so infuriates you that you find yourself (most uncharacteristically) using foul language?'

★　★　★

Most retired couples laugh at this story because something like it may have happened to them. It is comforting to realize that your troubles are shared by others; including those who have had a long and happy marriage.

It is even more comforting to find that the problems of togetherness can be laughable, as well as trying; and that this often makes for happy endings. Sheila's friend couldn't help being amused; and neither could Max. When his wife admitted her bad language to him, he fell about laughing; but it also convinced him that, one way or another, her Tuesday afternoons must be kept sacred.

Our research brought out another encouraging fact. The overdose of togetherness can end up as a big plus; not the minus it threatens to be in the early days of retirement. The career which carries one of the lowest risks of divorce is farming. A farmer and his wife really do spend their married years together. Most days they eat all their meals together. It is unusual for them to spend an evening, let alone a night, apart.

At the other end of the divorce scale come the marriages of showbiz stars, travelling salesmen, high-ranking executives, just about anyone whose way of life makes for periods of separation between husbands and wives. Divorce rates rocket.

Jackie Onassis found that her first marriage worked best when her husband became President of the United States. As an up and coming politician he had been racing here, there and everywhere. She said it was like being married to a whirlwind. But a President does much of his work in the White House – in effect, at home. It was not unusual for the children to crawl under John Kennedy's desk while he was working. Not unusual for him and Jackie to keep meeting up during the day.

The same is true of Queen Elizabeth and Prince Philip. The Prince once described their home at Buckingham Palace as, '... the flat above the shop.' This is where much of the work, involving them both, goes on. Many of their official engagements are taken together, both at home and overseas. Certainly the result appears to be a close and happy marriage.

Less grandly, we can cite the case of an ex-sailor and his wife who came close to divorce because, as he told us, 'We just didn't see enough of each other. When I came home it was like two strangers getting together; and it didn't work.' But everything changed when he left the Navy and the two set up a small restaurant together. The result, they agreed, was a very different relationship – much happier and much more stable.

Most couples we interviewed went along with Sam Harris's verdict that 'all day, every day, together' is going too far. If marital foul weather is to be avoided, some privacy is vital. Some separate activities are all to the good. This is particularly true in the first years of retirement when the adjustment to fifty-five weekly hours of togetherness, compared to eleven, causes the biggest upsets.

But whether one is talking about a farmer or a President, a sailor or a Queen, retired couples can be assured that togetherness can work.

It may produce some unexpected problems for you and your spouse. But after all of our interviews with retired men and their wives we can assure you that togetherness does work for almost every retired couple.

The years ahead can be the best of all.

★ ★ ★ ★

A NEW PROBLEM — AN OLD ANSWER

Some advice to wives who think that their retirement marriage
Has gone seriously amiss –
One thing that can still solve more marital problems than an international convention of marriage counsellors is
A warm, sexy kiss.

★ ★ ★ ★

2
Morning

Do you agree as to the importance of the critical 10?

ONE of our pleasures in working on this book has been the discovery of interesting ideas that many of our interviewees had already created to make their retirement marriages more satisfactory.

Perhaps the most intriguing was one mentioned by both men and women at all stages of their retired relationship – from several who had only been retired a few months, to one couple who had had a successful retirement marriage for over 24 years.

The idea concerned the importance of mornings.

And Bill and Donna S. thought that it was not just the morning that was important; it was the very first ten minutes that they were in each other's company every morning.

As Bill told us, 'Just after I retired we had some good days together – and some bad days, Not real bad – but bad enough to make us discuss afterwards why some days were so much better than others.

'Then it dawned on us. We figured out that on those mornings when we were first together after getting up – usually in the kitchen putting breakfast together – and when we greeted each other cheerfully, smiled a bit, mentioned something pleasant that perhaps we had heard on the radio news, even a minor compliment – on those days everything used to go swimmingly, all day long. We are now both conscious of those first ten minutes together and what we have come to call our "critical 10".'

Other couples have not been quite as specific but many stressed that when they did start the day with up-beat thoughts and conversation, the whole day went much better.

Mabel S. told us frankly, 'We now agree not to make any negative observations, any complaints, until mid-morning when we can handle them better. We even have sort of a silly understanding that when the weather is too wet or too hot or too something – we try to come out with some positive observation like, "The rain will certainly do the lawn a world of good."

'We recognize that sometimes we sound a little peculiar but it has become a bit of a game that we have played for years; with the prize, 99% of the time, of a pleasant day together.'

Of course, and very much on the other hand, we talked with couples who swore that they never said a word to each other for several hours each morning. (Winston Churchill is reputed after retirement to have had an agreement with his wife, Clementine, not to speak to each other at all until lunchtime.)

Even though we were not 100% sympathetic, we sensed that when a retired couple did have a mutual understanding on this point – with both partners agreeing completely – the rest of the day could be most satisfactory. There are people who take an extraordinarily long time in 'waking up' and it is probably asking too much to implore them to be bright and cheerful even before the coffee is brewed.

However, if one or the other of you – or best of all, both of you – feel that the morning is a fine time of day, and if you can

produce a smile, even a faint one, before you sit down for your cereal, we think that it is worth a conscious try to cheer your partner in some way. The couples that do work at it seem to reap wonderful benefits.

In our written questionnaires we asked each husband and wife to give us the three 'house rules' they thought should be made to improve marital relationships.

Quite a few of these 'house rules' related to the morning. For example:

DON'T TELL ME ANY BAD NEWS UNTIL AFTER BREAKFAST.

And, from a husband:

IF ANYTHING HAS TO BE FIXED AROUND THE HOUSE DON'T MENTION IT BEFORE 10AM.

And, from a wife:

TO KEEP ME PLEASANT AT BREAKFAST, DON'T MENTION MONEY.

As these suggested 'house rules' show, the subject of morning is uppermost in many retirement marriages. We began to think that 'the critical 10' was a lot more critical than we had ever thought.

One unfortunate retired wife told us that she often dreaded meeting her husband of a morning as he always aired at least one complaint, often more, on greeting her at breakfast. From 'I didn't sleep at all well last night' to 'You forgot to call the plumber yesterday'. And 'Did you hear that racket the kids upstairs made last night?' to 'I feel rotten – my damned arthritis.'

All true – but to have him arrive with a long face and negative thoughts practically every day in the year seemed to her to be most inappropriate, to say the least. She confided to us that she considered it not as his 'Good Morning' but rather as his 'Good Moaning'. But she never made this accurate observation to her husband.

Perhaps she should.

There is no such thing as a 'good' moaning.

3
Repeating Stories

If I have told you this one before, don't stop me!

In the great majority of our interviews where we were talking separately with a wife, or a husband, we heard the words, 'I wish Jack – or Jane – or Henry – or Sue – wouldn't tell the same story over and over again.'

In a very few cases this meant that wives were tired of hearing their husband's jokes for the umpteenth time. But we were surprised as we went along to find that oft-repeated jokes were only a minor factor in this problem. (Evidently, those wives who had husbands with a talent for telling jokes had developed something of a defence mechanism in that they, the wives, had nurtured the ability to forget the punch lines and therefore could laugh heartily on hearing the same joke again. And again. And again.)

What turned out to be the major problem was straight stories – not necessarily humorous, but interesting stories – or so the teller thought. For example, Jack D. said to us, 'If I hear Martha's story again about her visit to her 98-year-old aunt in Leeds, I just couldn't take it. It was of interest when she first told it, but not ten years later.'

Later that same day it was Martha's turn to tell us, 'Every time we meet someone new, Jack regales them with the story of the time I was stopped by the police on the High Street and accused of soliciting. I must have heard it a thousand times – and I suspect some of our friends have heard it about as often.'

We did not sense that there was much of a repeating-stories problem when a wife and a husband were at home alone. In these cases, for the most part, the teller could remember that he or she had already reported the details to the partner. But the problem became rampant when other friends or acquaintances were present. (In truth, the story of Martha's 98-year-old aunt was quite interesting when she told it to us. With Jack almost obviously squirming in his chair.)

But everyone has favourite stories. We are sure that all of us recognize the moment when we start to tell some friends a story that we know that our partner has heard all too often. The usual apology that precedes many stories, 'Jack has heard me tell this story a hundred times. But . . .' doesn't make the story any more interesting to Jack.

The alternative introduction is, 'Jack, why don't you get us all a beer while I tell them about my 98-year-old aunt in Leeds who still drove a car.' This, at least, gets him out of earshot during the telling.

Another aspect of the repeating stories problem came up often in our interviews. It was referred to by some as 'stretching the truth', by others as 'embroidering', and still others as 'exaggerating'. Jill G. put it this way, 'All of Oscar's stories are at least based on the truth but in telling, and retelling, them over the years he keeps changing a minor detail here and there – like reporting he was going fifty miles an hour when he fell off his water skis. When I first heard the story, he was going twenty. And I admit I have found myself doing much the same. Just last week I recall telling some friends at lunch that I remember as a little girl when the temperature in our village went down to 30 below. I hope that no one bothered to check the old weather reports.'

It was generally agreed that this tendency to add a little something to all of our stories was an attempt to make them more interesting – especially as we, the tellers, had heard ourselves repeat the story so often that it was becoming uninteresting even to ourselves.

There is not much we can recommend on this subject except for all of us to be aware that, in every couple, one or the other partner, usually both, are exposed to the spouse's favourite stories many, many times, and we should try to limit the repeats to some degree.

Further, we should all remember that when we start a story and we have someone present who has heard the details before – often many times before – we should stick fairly close to the original facts.

Oh yes; one point we can certainly recommend is to resist at all costs the temptation to interrupt the story-teller with comments like, 'Darling, you know that ever since weather records have been kept, the lowest temperature ever recorded in Norfolk was 8 below.' Or, 'Come on Jack, that old outboard the kids used for water skiing wouldn't go more than 20 miles an hour even going downhill.'

Such comments might make the story more truthful. But they won't make a marriage more serene.

A PS FROM PHOEBE

One of the nicest and kindest contributions a wife or a husband can make is to say when there are other people around, 'Do tell them that story – or that joke – about . . .' It does not really matter what the story or the joke is about. The fact that your partner gives you the opportunity to tell something that he or she knows is a favourite story of yours – even though it has been heard many times before – says a lot for marriage.

4

Physical Affection

. . . and it doesn't have to be SEX

THIS is a fundamental issue. Moreover, it is one where the views of the woman and the views of the man do not reach an easy compromise.

For this reason we have decided to make an exception and write our separate viewpoints rather than make a joint statement. At the end you will find that we have reached what we think is a constructive conclusion because both of us feel the subject is so important.

It is, perhaps, the most important in the whole book. And our objective, as stated in the Introduction, is not just to expose problems but to suggest ways of dealing with them. As Joe says, 'Ladies first.'

So here is Phoebe:

It is agreed that a small baby wants more than food and clinical care. He or she thrives on the warmth and comfort of another human body, and the need persists even when the child grows older and more independent. The toddler who bruises a head or grazes a knee wants, more than anything, a loving lap and a pair of arms. 'Kiss it better' remains an irreplaceable treatment.

Freud may have seen sex implications in all this. But to most of us it is a simple and natural case of physical affection, and it may be provided by men as well as women. The stimulus of sexual contact is something different.

No one denies, of course, that the stimulus of sex plays a

massive part in our marriages. But two important questions remain. Does physical affection between husband and wife have to be sexual, every time? Is kissing, hugging, holding hands unacceptable unless an orgasm is in view?

It has made me a little sad to find out how many wives felt that the answers to both questions should be 'NO' – but they added that they were not sure their husbands would agree. As Joy S. wrote to me:

> We've had a good marriage. But certain things change as you get older and, now that we're retired, I do notice – more and more – a lack in our relationship.
>
> Jim has never been a demonstrative person. I remember, he was always a bit embarrassed to kiss his own mother, and even more embarrassed to kiss mine! And now the same attitude is coming out towards me.
>
> So long as we had a busy sex life, and indeed a busy life in general, I don't think I noticed or worried. But one's sex life is bound to become less active; and he seems to feel that this makes physical contact unnecessary.
>
> It's not that we have stopped loving each other. If I dropped dead tomorrow, I truly believe he'd be devastated. But is it unreasonable of me to want more show of affection? Even without sex?

This is a typical question, and one that does seem to come more from women than from men. The problem may have surfaced earlier in married life; but it's obviously going to become more important, more noticeable as the sex drive slows down. And it is obvious, too, that retirement may make matters worse. When couples start spending so much more time together, any 'minus' in a relationship is going to be extra difficult.

The wife with young children will probably give and receive physical affection from them. In retirement, she's going to rely more on her husband. Who else? As another female correspondent wrote, 'You really hate to feel that physical affection has to be sex or nothing. With many men, you may end up with nothing. Not good when that man is the most important person in your life.'

Physical Affection

Am I being brainwashed? Are retired wives making too much of this?

I have talked this over with psychologists and found that, by and large, they have sympathy with the woman's point of view. No, they say, wives aren't imagining things. Many husbands, as they grow older, *do* become physically undemonstrative, almost like young boys. And the comparison with young boys can be very revealing.

The phrase 'second childhood' does not have to mean senility. Perfectly intelligent and sensible men can revert to some aspects of their boyhood *and* remain intelligent and sensible. No contradictions here. Just an emotional throwback.

In general, young boys become embarrassed by physical affection much more easily than young girls. They wriggle off laps. They dislike being told to kiss Aunt Emily. It's manly to play rough games, sissy to hold hands and cuddle. That's for the girls.

Perhaps that's true. Sisters are happier to stay on laps, hold hands, snuggle and cuddle. They may pass through awkward teenage phases, but physical affection usually remains a fact of life. A 13-year-old-boy will shrink from oohing and aahing over a small baby. A girl of the same age will take that kind of loving in her stride. She did it with her dolls or her puppy or her kitten, and it still seems natural.

Sex is a great leveller, and the balance may indeed tip the other way. The young man who falls in love often desires physical contact more urgently than the girl; and this desire can continue through much of his life. But we are talking about retired couples, where sex is less overpowering. And this is where the boyhood embarrassment, the 'that's for girls' attitude begins to reassert itself. All right for two women to hug and kiss each other when they meet, but don't expect two men to go in for that kind of thing. (Unless they're Arabs.) From there, it's a shortish step for the older man to decide that it isn't appropriate to hug and kiss women either. A peck on the cheek, perhaps. No more.

It wouldn't hurt, either, for the man to remember how nice it was to cuddle his own small children – sons as well as daughters. Most fathers sense and understand a child's need for physical affection and are happy to provide it.

On this whole subject, I cannot help sympathizing with the woman's side. In almost every in-depth interview I have had with wives who are otherwise enjoying a retirement marriage, the subject comes up in varying degrees. I have concluded that the French 'Vive la difference' goes much too far when it comes to the occasional, quiet bit of loving physical affection. On this point, I wish that there was not all that much difference between women and men – particularly at this stage of their married lives.

I believe that women *do* have an enduring need for physical affection. More enduring than sex. It does not have to be a big deal, and it does not have to happen every day. A reassuring arm around the waist in a crowd. An enthusiastic hug for birthdays, Christmas, meeting after a time apart – or for no reason at all.

Or just a husband reaching out for a wife's hand when a favourite tune comes on. This all might sound, '. . . as corny as Kansas in August' but does that matter? Especially if it makes a wife happier – and a marriage more pleasant.

So, I think the clear message, particularly from older wives, is that the man who reverts to boyhood and decides that physical affection is sissy and superfluous – and just for females – should grow up a second time. And think again.

Now, Joe, I've had my say. It's your turn.

So here's Joe:

OK Phoebe. That's an interesting story. And I'll do my best to grow up a second time.

But before I do, I should tell you that I have discussed your piece with various colleagues and friends – all male – all over 60.

Speaking broadly we do not have much argument with many of your points. And we do agree that most wives do desire more casual physical affection than most husbands provide. However, we think that there may be a basic reason why this very-much-to-be-regretted situation exists.

Now hear me out. Because, right off, I am going to bring up sex; and though this is not the same as casual physical affection, the two are related.

So, don't sit there shaking your head and saying to yourself,

26

'Sex is not what I was writing about. My concern had to do with the occasional hug, holding hands, the casual kiss. Not sex *per se*.'

Honestly, Phoebe, I understand that. But let me continue.

As every one knows, the sex drive in a man continues as he matures, let's say, into his 60's and 70's – and beyond. On the other hand we are told that most women's interest in sex tapers off after menopause. So, as casual physical affection is certainly related in many ways to sex, many men reason that since a woman's interest in the latter has declined, her interest in the former is also on the wane.

I am sure that you will say that this is bad reasoning – and it may be. (However, to try to get men to understand that as your interest in sex goes *down*, your interest in casual physical affection goes *up*, is really a hard sale to make.)

But men do not have the exclusive rights to bad reasoning. I think women do it too. They appear to reason that since a woman's interest in sex declines, her husband's need for it also declines. They seem to think that a decline in frequency indicates that the sex drive is disappearing.

Wrong.

Now to connect the two – casual affection and sex. And I hope to make an observation or two that will help all of us who have a small, or a large, problem in this area.

We men could claim that if a wife wants to encourage the former, she should encourage the latter – and thereby discredit the male argument that she has lost, after menopause, interest in both kinds of physical activity.

I know, Phoebe, you are about to say that if men want more interest in sex, they should expand their casual physical affection. And you are no doubt correct. But before we men rest our case, let me report what one older husband asked me to suggest to you. Namely, that you query all wives who are concerned with a lack of casual physical affection with one very specific and very personal question.

And that question is, 'How long has it been since you seduced your husband?'

And don't accept an answer from any woman that she has lost her powers of seduction. If she thinks this, that's why she has the problem of the missing casual affection on the part of her husband.

I am absolutely certain that most men consider their wives seductive – especially when they want to be. It is a minor detail that today, perhaps, the wife's figure is not as good as it was some years ago, or that her hair is grey. or that she has added a pound or two. (While on this subject, I can assure you that all men recognize that they no longer have the thin, handsome, virile bodies they once possessed.) However, a marriage that has enjoyed a satisfying, even exciting, sexual relationship at any point always has the basis for a renewal whenever both partners are willing to encourage it.

So, Phoebe, ask my friend's question of your women friends. Perhaps it will indicate a solution to their problem concerning the lack of casual physical affection from their husbands.

And if, at the same time, we husbands work, as you recommend, at preventing ourselves from reverting to boyhood when we were disdainful of showing our emotions, we might see a resurgence of hand-holding, the unexpected hug, and the surprise kiss.

And even more.

Let's hope so.

OUR CONCLUSION

We have discussed this subject verbally for some months. But now that we have both written down our viewpoints in black and white, we have been surprised to find out how much better we understand each other.

(Perhaps there is a moral here for our readers who may sometimes find that mutually writing things down can work better than lengthy conversation. Conversation has a habit of becoming acrimonious, particularly when it is a subject where both parties feel very strongly.)

Phoebe now accepts that her woman's viewpoint did not give enough importance to sex. She stresses that while she was talking primarily about physical affection, she acknowledges that sex has to come in. Her conclusion is that women should stop and ask themselves, 'Have I done enough for my husband in the sex department? Can we expect to have it both ways? Can we give him a bit of a brush off sexually, and then expect to be gently holding hands at midnight?'

She suggests that this is something a wife may wish to talk out with her husband. But even if the wife feels embarrassed and would like to avoid a discussion, she should think it over herself. And see what she can do.

It could be, as Joe says, that more physical affection would follow.

Joe admits that, in recent years, he had not realized how much he was beginning to behave like he did when he was thirteen. That was a time when a football had much more appeal than a girl – and any display of physical affection was the exclusive preserve of females of any age. (It turns out he did have an Aunt Emily and he can still remember how his heart sank when he was urged, by his mother, to kiss her.)

His conclusion is that men should be aware of this tendency, and that an older husband should not emulate an inhibited, insensitive, thirteen year old. And unless he does something about it, and quickly, he could spend what's left of his life sleeping with a football.

A final story. Many years ago a well-known personality, a widower, aged 80, married a woman in her 70's. An over-zealous journalist while interviewing him asked, 'Sir, why did you get married at your age? Sex was certainly not a factor.'

His answer was, 'At age ten I thought that the ultimate in pleasure was a big dish of chocolate ice cream. Nothing could give as much pleasure. Later I married and found out about sex – and ice cream was forgotten. I had discovered, I thought, true ecstasy. But now that I have found someone with whom I have a complete, gentle, uncomplicated understanding, I have found something that surpasses, by far, both ice cream *and* sex.'

Then he added, 'Off the record, I still also enjoy both – occasionally.'

The advice from both of us: PLEASE, PLEASE DO NOT GIVE UP ON THIS ONE. There are many important factors in a retirement marriage. But we truly believe that this could be one of the most important of all.

5
Meal Habits

Do you eat with a newspaper, TV, or a person?

EARLY on in our research we talked at length with a couple whom we both sensed were enjoying an excellent retirement relationship. However, we were amazed to learn that the husband and the wife each read newspapers all through breakfast – and through lunch – and through much of their evening meal – all of which they ate together.

When questioned as to whether they thought that this was an excessive concentration on reading – and a very limiting activity for communications between the two of them – we were greeted with spirited arguments from both that, to the contrary, they felt this helped bring new interests to their marriage.

They pointed out that, while they spent most of the time with the papers propped up in front of them, they did have conversational interchanges whenever one, or the other, found something considered of mutual interest. In subsequent interviews we found other couples who had similar mealtime reading, and conversation, habits.

A typical comment was, 'We are not great talkers and after more than forty years we've said everything we know to each other. Newspapers may not be the most stimulating method to widen our horizons, but they help.'

As we talked with more and more couples we found this topic of mealtime habits was one on which our respondents had firm opinions. For instance, many could not believe that any couple read newspapers that intensely.

However, when we asked them what they did at meals, the

answer usually was, 'We watch TV.' They were critical of the newspaper readers, but thought it perfectly acceptable to watch TV. Most claimed that it was the news that they watched, but many readily confessed to viewing a variety of other programmes.

Those couples who told us that they never, ever ate alone at home without the company of either newspapers or television were in a distinct minority.

Incidentally, when we asked about reading books, rather than newspapers, we found very few men, or women, who admitted that they were book readers while dining. The reason was that when mealtime readers are engrossed in a book they are, in a serious sense, not at the same table as their wives or husbands. They are with the characters in the book. And the readers of books would also resent the informal interruptions that newspapers and TV allow, and indeed encourage.

We should note that there was a certain embarrassment on the part of many couples when they did tell us that they either read or watched TV, at meals together. Many seemed to be somewhat ashamed to admit it.

Some couples are blessed with the ability to talk to each other 21 meals a week – and in between too. But they are few and far between. For the rest of us, we recommend that we should take advantage of today's informative, and often interesting, media that can, at times, open new windows on our world.

If you are one of those couples who find it natural to read or watch TV, or listen to the radio, at meals, don't worry about it. We can assure you that you are in the company of many happily married families.

A caution, however.

Like any habit if it gets out of hand it can be a problem. So do not let newspapers or TV dominate your meals. Interrupt them often with comments or observations – or disagreements with what you are reading or watching.

They are much better than disagreements with each other.

★ ★ ★ ★

WEATHER REPORT

'Marriage problems can be dire
When a man and wife retire;
Specially when his vigour wanes,
Specially when his wife complains
Specially, specially when IT RAINS!'

Mark Lytton

★ ★ ★ ★

6
Over and Above the Call of Duty

How you can get the outstanding awards.

THE military award their heroes with a medal for action 'over and above the call of duty'.

While the world of business doesn't give medals, it does give salary rises and titles and other goodies to employees who do something unexpected – unexpectedly good, that is.

Employers do not find it very difficult to find people who will do precisely what they are told to do, but no more. They find it very difficult to hire men and women who will do things 'over and above'. It is also equally difficult to find men and women who add a dimension to their retirement marriage with activities over and above the normal marriage expectancy.

All marriages – retirement or earlier – thrive on those occasional activities that are totally unexpected.

But where husbands and wives have been together for many years, those special actions are particularly needed to prevent a marriage from falling into an ever more stultifying routine. We have found that those marriages where one, or both, partners work at doing something 'over and above the call of duty' are far and away the most successful.

So, what are some of these extraordinary, 'over and above', actions?

The answers, we found, were almost as numerous as there were respondents. Everything from a husband's quiet invitation, 'Let's go out for dinner tonight,' to a wife's, 'I know it's not your birthday, but I baked you one of those special chocolate cakes you love.'

Or, 'Here, my love, is a rose for you,' to 'How would you like me to bring you breakfast in bed this morning?' Or, 'I'll cook dinner tonight.' Or a wife's comment while her husband is watching football on TV, 'Don't get up when you want a beer. I'll bring it for you.'

Both of us were amazed at the simplicity of some of the stories. One wife said, 'I had been doing a lot of baking and the sink was stacked with dirty pans. After I had everything in the oven, I left to make a few telephone calls. On my return I found that my husband had come in from the garden, saw the dirty pans, washed, dried, and put them all away. I was pleased beyond belief.'

While a husband reported that his wife knew he had a favourite brand of pipe tobacco that he had been unable to find for months. One very rainy afternoon she returned home with three packages of the elusive product. He then discovered she had spent two hours, and tramped to eight stores, before she found it. He was, of course, delighted. And he admitted that the fact she was dripping wet made him feel that this small gift was really over and above the call of duty.

The odd thing was that no one mentioned such comments as, 'Here's a new bracelet,' or 'Let's take a trip to Florida,' as qualifying for consideration. It was always something relatively small that was reported as being meaningful.

So money seldom seems to enter into it – or if money is involved, it is not the money that is impressive, it is the thought that went into it.

One wife – albeit quite a wealthy one – told us that she had been complaining for months of feeling 'shut in' even though she admitted that she was shut into a lovely home with a nice garden. But she never seemed to get out of it.

The husband saw an opportunity for something unexpected. He bought her an old bird cage, gilded it, and made a sort of stuffed bird which he put on the perch. In its beak he placed a short poem he had written on the theme 'A bird in a gilded cage' – plus theatre tickets for two during the next four weeks.

A diamond tiara would not have been more welcome. She was delighted.

In *Alice in Wonderland* Humpty Dumpty invented the idea of 'unbirthdays'. On real birthdays, at Christmas or on anniversaries, something extra is already expected so it is more difficult to conjure up ideas that are 'over and above'.

However, 'unbirthdays' can certainly spice up a marriage. A gift, or some action, no matter how small, is 'over and above' because it is totally unexpected. And the advantage of unbirthdays is that there are 364 of them every year.

Tomorrow could be your spouse's unbirthday – and therefore an opportunity for you to do something a little over and above the normal routine.

It could even be today.

A PS FROM PHOEBE

Joe is reticent to include one of the best 'over and above' presents to a wife that I have heard of. He is reticent because he was the one who did it for his wife Audrey.

One summer weekend they had invited some people to stay – and more were expected for meals on both Saturday and Sunday. Early that week he told Audrey that she was *not* – absolutely *not* – going to be allowed in the kitchen from 5pm on the Friday until the following Monday morning.

When the guests arrived they found a large notice which read, 'KITCHEN UNDER NEW MANAGEMENT THIS WEEK-END. Don't expect the usual miracles.' And Joe, with lots of help from the guests, prepared the (simple) meals, saw to it that all the washing up was done, arranged for Audrey's breakfast to be served in her bed, and her drink each evening delivered, on a tray, in the living room.

And for some 60 consecutive hours Audrey never appeared once in the kitchen – something she had never done before in their entire married life – and probably hasn't done since.

It was certainly 'over and above' and Audrey remembers it to this day.

I hope my husband Ted reads this!

★ ★ ★ ★

AMOR VINCIT OMNIA

Perhaps our most forthright interview was with a 69 year old woman who, at the end of our interview, volunteered this report.
'Recently I apologized to our Vicar because one Sunday we missed his usual early Communion. I said I was sorry but my husband and I had made love that morning and we just stayed in bed. He smiled and said, "Never apologize for that. After all Communion and love are much the same thing. But", he added, with a large grin, "don't forget there are six other days in the week."'

★ ★ ★ ★

7

Who's Boss?

And what's the difference between being boss and being bossy?

WHEN, in our interviews, we asked the question, 'Who do you think is boss in your family?' we received a wide variety of answers plus a great deal of thought-provoking observations.

One couple, being interviewed together, both instantly responded 'Not me!' Another pair, this time being interviewed separately, also both used exactly the same words, 'I guess I'm the boss.'

The problem seemed to vary greatly based on the situation during all those years when one or both were working. Michael and Wendy J., now both almost eighty, said that they ran a small restaurant during their working life. Michael was, without question, the boss in the kitchen, while Wendy ran the front of the operation, including the money.

They insisted there never was a problem until they sold the restaurant ten years ago, and they found themselves both trying to be boss in their home. They think they have, at last, arrived at a solution to the 'Who's boss?' problem, but they made no bones about it that it was not easy.

The same was true of Helen and John K. He was a solicitor with a small office and his wife was his secretary. Their arrangement was clear cut. He was the boss in the office. She at home. They were now in the first year of his retirement and admitted they had many things still to work out.

Mary D. did not work after she and Jack raised their five children. They both agreed that when Jack was working full time, and Mary was at home, he was certainly the boss. Everything revolved around him and his job.

When he retired, Jack said that he would turn over the boss duties to Mary – and she agreed. Now Jack says he is enjoying every minute of it. 'I haven't made a major decision in two years,' he reported. 'And a major decison would be whether to buy new tyres for the car, redecorate a bathroom, or to go to Spain for a holiday. Oh yes, I do make the decision as to whether I will have eggs or cereal for breakfast, but not much more. After forty years of being boss, I appreciate my loss of authority; because I no longer have any responsibility – other than to make a quiet suggestion from time to time. But only when asked.'

Another couple have solved their problem – at least when they are on holiday – by agreeing that one day the husband will make every necessary decision. When they are touring, he decides what they will do all day; where they'll go, where they'll eat, and he has to pick out the B&B for the night. He is in full charge. He cannot even ask his wife, 'Does this look like a good place to stay?'

The next day she has total responsibility. Further, they have agreed never to complain if the other's decisions turn out to be less than, perfect. Not even, after dining, an observation like, 'That was a poor meal.' The day's decision-maker can say it, but not the partner.

Interestingly, they say, after many holidays with the every-other-day-being-boss policy, they enjoy it much more when the other is making the decisions. The wife commented, 'I'm always much more relaxed. Even though one day recently Will insisted that we spend the whole day at a cricket match. Which certainly is not my cup of tea. But on the other hand I've taken him to more gardens than he ever wanted to see.'

We should report that quite a few couples feel that the 'Who's boss?' question is not a factor in their marriage. Fortunately, they have developed some kind of wonderful understanding – and they are to be envied.

All in all the answer is not concerned with 'Who's boss?'. When we found a problem it seemed to originate with one partner or the other being too bossy. In married life, as in business, a good boss tends not to be too bossy. We often sensed that certain wives

— and let us be crystal clear on this subject — and certain husbands — took great pleasure in issuing specific orders and making direct statements when a soft, quiet suggestion would suffice.

It is human nature to want to be a boss to some degree. Even though we may deny it, we all prefer to make decisions rather than abide by those made by someone else. It is true that we often want to have our partner make a decision on some subject in which we are not interested. Like, 'I wish Agnes would decide what I should give her for a birthday present,' or 'When we go out, I wish Jack would decide the restaurant we will eat in.'

We start out in life being bossed by our parents and our teachers. When we go to work we are immediately aware that we have a boss — usually several layers of them. Until the day we retire most of us have never been in a position where we do not have a direct boss. So it is understandable that the 'Who's boss?' situation often arises at that time.

So our suggestion is — be aware of the possible problem, Talk to your partner and develop a workable solution.

And above all, don't be bossy.

8

Is Your Spouse an 'Eccentric'?

... or a character or a non-conformist or just unconventional?

IN our interviews we kept running into couples who, when asked whether their partner was eccentric in any way, answered with a resounding 'Yes'.

Many answered much like Mabel D. who said, 'Yes, I am sure that some of our friends and many of our neighbours think Jack is an eccentric.'

When we asked why, Mabel went on to say, 'Well, when the weather is pleasant Jack takes the dog for a walk at six every morning and walks around the block in an old bathrobe and always wears an old beret he found in France in World War II. He looks dreadful. I would hate to be seen with him.'

But that, in our opinion, is not as eccentric as Blanche M. whose husband Bill reported, 'My wife keeps our house nice enough but the beat-up old estate car she drives hasn't been washed in five years – if then. Further, she is a pretty good amateur sculptress and keeps all her work and materials in the car permanently, and that includes two old dustbins filled with I don't know what, at least a hundredweight of old newspapers, dozens of half-empty cans of paint – and she's not a painter – a stuffed sparrowhawk which she bought years ago and has never left the car – just to name a few of the items.'

When Blanche was up changing her clothes Bill showed us the car. He was right. Only an eccentric would dare take it to a local supermarket. We even saw the disintegrating ancient straw hat she always insists on wearing when driving.

We should explain that some husbands and wives did not go so

far as to use the word 'eccentric' but did admit their spouse was something of a 'character' or a 'non-conformist' or 'quite unconventional'. You will be glad to learn that no one said their spouse was out-and-out 'crazy'.

(Joe says he is forced to admit that we found many more wives who thought their retired husbands were eccentric than vice-versa. He tried to make the excuse that men were more considerate than wives in reporting on this subject but the evidence is clear. Men are more willing than women to be considered eccentric.)

Further, a high percentage of the comments about a husband being eccentric had to do with their clothes. From, 'On those few occasions when Henry gets dressed up he insists on wearing a day-glo red bow tie,' to, 'My husband somehow acquired years ago an American baseball cap – the New York Yankees – and every time he goes out of the house it's on his head – whether he is going to mow to lawn or take me out to dinner.'

There is little doubt that as men and women get older we all allow ourselves to be become a bit eccentric. When we were in our teens we were very concerned as to what our contemporaries thought of us. We all probably did some things our parents thought eccentric but our actions were, we thought, the current style.

Later in life we are not so concerned with what others think of the things we do. We now have more confidence. If people think we are a little eccentric just because we wear a day-glo red bow tie, or a baseball cap, or walk down the street in a grubby bathrobe, so what?

Psychologists tell us that most, but not all, eccentrics act the way they do in order to get attention – whether it is dying their hair pink when they are fifteen or driving a disreputable car when they are seventy-two. They suggest that, in some cases, a little more attention from a retired spouse might make an eccentric a little less eccentric. Who knows? If it is a problem in your marriage it might be worth a try.

As long as your eccentricity does not get to a point where you estrange your friends, we concluded that no harm is done – and perhaps even some benefits accrue to a retirement marriage.

We were sure that Bill – whose wife Blanche drives the unsightly estate car – is sometimes a little embarrassed by having her 'dust cart' parked in their drive. However they seem to have a quite satisfactory marriage on other counts. As did almost all of the other couples where one or the other – occasionally both – thought that their spouse was eccentric in some way.

The key seems to be in keeping the limit of eccentricity within reasonable bounds – and not letting it move on to where one is considered 'crazy'. We have read about an older man who started collecting and saving massive amounts of newspapers and magazines until they were stacked high in every room in their flat. In the end the couple had to move out and sleep rough.

That's going too far.

9
Projects

When you wake up in the morning
  And there's nothing much to do
But think about the weather
  And reflect upon the view.

There's breakfast, lunch, and dinner
  And a drink or two – or more:
But nothing looks so very bright,
  And most things are a bore.

When all the post is bills (and bills)
  And kids next door are bawling;
Your wife has got a headache
  Your arthritis is appalling.

When there you sit, just wondering
  What life is all about:
A PROJECT is an object
  You just CANNOT DO WITHOUT!

ONE authority on projects is the former American President, Jimmy Carter. He hadn't planned to retire. He and his wife, Rosalynn, hoped for another term in the White House, but it was not to be.

Stepping out of any job is seldom easy. To step down from such high office on short notice must be particularly difficult. The fact that it was done unwillingly cannot have helped.

But the Carters have survived and have, jointly, written a book. It is titled, 'Everything to Gain'. With a sub-title, 'Making the Most of the Rest of Your Life'.

Whatever one's views on his performance as a President, or one's views on her as the First Lady, it is impossible to do anything but admire the way they rebuilt their life together. Very much together. It illustrates the importance of PROJECTS in the later days of life and marriage.

In another topic in this book we have suggested – perhaps to the horror of our more house-proud readers – that PROJECTS should take precedence over the humdrum household chores. But we feel the subject should be explored further because it is crucial.

Our correspondents do not agree on everything, but we have yet to find one who rejected outside interests as undesirable. Some admitted they had not been successful at finding them, which they regretted. All said that a husband and wife, living Round the Clock with little to interest them, was a recipe for marital disharmony.

We have to admit that not everyone has the physical energy of the Carters. They became involved in a project called 'Habitat for Humanity'. The object was to renovate old buildings, with the help of unpaid volunteers, and make them into reasonable homes for people who would otherwise be homeless.

The volunteers were not only unpaid; most of them, including the Carters, were also unskilled in this kind of work.

Once Rosalynn found herself nailing down a new floor, just after she had told Jimmy, 'I'll do anything but hammer. I don't think I can use a hammer.' But she did. At first it took her 20 strokes for each nail. At the end of the week, she could do it in 5.

She summed it up, 'If I can be a carpenter, dear reader, you can be anything you want to be.'

Jimmy's comment says a lot about their marriage. 'My wife is never more beautiful than when her face is covered with black smut from scraping burned ceiling joists; and streaked with sweat from carrying sheets of plywood from the street up to the fourth floor.'

It underlines, of course. the advantages of a shared PRO-JECT. Jimmy worked alongside his wife. He would have been less enthusiastic if he had stayed home to feed the cat, walk the dog, and cook the dinner.

Projects

In England, John Profumo was another case of sudden, enforced retirement. After his much publicised affair with Christine Keeler he found himself out of politics, with no job of any kind.

A friend of Phoebe's lived opposite his London home and could look across into the ex-Minister's study. After the great drama, Profumo seemed to establish a regular routine. Every morning he would sit at his desk – for hours – looking into space, doing nothing.

One suspects that this sad routine had something to do with the wife who had loyally supported him throughout. He did not want *her* to think that he had nowhere to go, nothing to do.

As most people know, the story has a happy ending. Soon he found a PROJECT – and became an active social worker. Then there was no pretence about having nowhere to go, nothing to do. His new life among the down-and-outs has been full and rewarding. We wish that he, like the Carters, would write a book describing what he has done.

But do not get us wrong!

We are not suggesting that all of us Senior Citizens should make a PROJECT of doing voluntary social work. There are thousands of other PROJECTS for you to select.

We have been absolutely delighted to talk with people, and hear from others, who have taken up PROJECTS of painting, tapestry, furniture restoration, writing, tree planting, wild flower gardens, dried flower arranging, sculpture, patchwork quilts, historical research, gliding (yes, gliding), scuba diving, or amateur operatic production. To name a few.

We especially liked the 77-year-old who told us that she and her husband had never known such perfect happiness until (jointly) they learned to train carrier pigeons.

It's never too late to take up something new. As the poem says,

'A PROJECT is an object
You just CANNOT DO WITHOUT.'

★ ★ ★ ★

A SEASONAL APPROACH

In a posh London Club two retired gentlemen were quietly talking.
The first asked discreetly, 'Could I ask, do you and your wife still do it?'
The second said, 'Yes.'
The first, more boldly, then asked, 'Are you a oncer or a twicer?'
The second responded. 'I'm a twicer.'
Then the first gentleman, very boldly, enquired, 'Would you mind telling me which one you prefer?'
To which the second's answer, after great thought, was, 'The one in the spring.'

★ ★ ★ ★

10
Getting Things Done

... or, how to win the war with Parkinson's Law.

'I really looked forward to retiring,' one of our women corres-pondents, who had had a high-powered job in advertising, wrote. 'Just the business of getting up early five days a week, hurrying off to the office, always in the rush hour, often in bad weather, seemed more and more uncongenial – even though I enjoyed the work.

'When I did retire it was like taking off a corset. At first there was a lovely feeling of relief. And I enjoyed being with my husband – but then I found I wasn't getting anything done.'

This, we found, was a common reaction from both men and women, and was one that was bound to have an effect on their marriage. Parkinson's Law:

THE LESS YOU HAVE TO DO, THE LONGER IT TAKES YOU TO DO IT

is alarmingly true. At the end of the day so many people look back and wonder, 'What did I do today?' And their answer is, 'Nothing worth mentioning. I just fiddled around.'

This was the problem with innumerable men, most women who had been working, and, surprisingly, with many full-time housewives who now had a husband at home all day. We had thought that this last group would not have the problem as their workload probably increased a bit. We concluded that the 'Getting things done' dilemma is not only related to retirement but also to the fact we are all getting a little older each year.

Many women reckoned that there is always something to be done in the kitchen. Washing up this, putting away that, sorting out bits of food, clearing the fridge, sweeping the floor . . . all before or after actually producing a meal. It takes forever, and the women told us it was most unstimulating; and they end the day with a gloomy sense of non-achievement; which can, amongst other things, make you irritable with your husband.

Men, we sensed, were better at rebuilding a routine. (Getting back into their corsets.) They learn how to get more into the day, and are also better at developing a new project that is stimulating and does give them a sense of achievement.

This could well be because men are not plagued with household trivia, lucky devils. If they wish to retreat to their garden or work-room to pursue a project, they can just set aside a whole morning. No interruptions. The wife, faced with laundry and beds and carpets and the everlasting kitchen, does not find it so easy.

The best advice we heard on the subject came from our friend Andrew Murray. He began by stressing the importance of specific projects for the wife, as well as the husband. He has much sympathy for the wife who retires from a lively job and finds herself something of a household drudge. She *must* have projects – something else to stimulate her.

Projects, of course, have to be the choice of each individual. But Murray's Law is:

PUT THE PROJECT BEFORE, NOT AFTER, THE
HOUSEHOLD CHORES

If you are going to write your sexy novel, work out new ways of raising money for the disabled or redesign your garden – *don't, don't* wait until you have cleared away the dishes, polished the furniture, or rung the plumber. Chores can wait; and if you do them first you will find that they always take all of your time.

More important, chores sap your creative energy. When finished, you don't feel like doing anything except sitting down for a cup of coffee and reading the newspaper. The project, whatever it is, goes by the board. Triumph of Parkinson's Law. Yet again.

Yes, chores have to be done; but they can be done remarkably fast when the time available is limited. Career girls will remember how they dashed home from the office, cleaned the flat, cooked dinner for eight – all in a very short time. No – it was not just a question of youthful energy. It was, we must repeat, a question of the time available.

The fact that there was so little time available in those days was what kept Parkinson's Law at bay.

The house-proud may find Murray's Law an alarming approach. Visions of overflowing sinks, dusty rooms, and unmade beds. But it does not have to be like that because no one is suggesting that the chores should not be done – or even skimped. It is a question of confining them within strict time limits.

The point of Murray's Law is that projects, unlike the laundry, can be postponed for months or years. Yet it is these projects, unlike the laundry, which get the adrenalin moving; and which, importantly, add a fillip to a retired day and a retired marriage.

That is why the projects should be given priority – and given it at a time of day when you feel most lively, most creative. Save the chores for when you are bored and tired and you will get through them much quicker.

There is no doubt that Parkinson's Law is all too true. But Murray's Law could be your answer.

A PS FROM JOE

Years ago I saw a display of the crests of many important English families. Most of the mottos were in Latin. Almost all were high-blown and had to do with honour, or truth, or liberty. One motto stood out. It was very down to earth. It consisted of just three words – only seven letters. If you were to have a crest, I recommend this motto. All it said was, 'DO IT NOW'.

11
Ingrained Habits

Good habits, bad habits, and plain old habitual habits.

'AT our age,' a woman in her 70's told us, 'we are mostly habits. Each morning I put on my slippers exactly the same way. I put precisely the same amount of toothpaste on the brush. And when Bill takes the dog out on the lead each morning they always go to the same tree. And we have a dozen trees the dog could choose from.'

Some habits we found were appreciated by the partner. Jack S. has put two lumps of sugar in his wife's coffee every morning since their honeymoon. Matthew W. has always enjoyed his wife's habit of whistling a tune as she makes breakfast. The tunes change, but the habit persists. And Martha S. told us she enjoys her husband's habit of standing up when she enters a room where he is sitting down. (She liked this habit, but she also reported on some she was not happy with.)

On the negative side, the stories of little habits that upset partners were widely varied, but they did have one common denominator. They were to us, outsiders, extremely trivial – but understandable.

Meg N. was annoyed because Bill always cleared his throat with a little cough before he spoke. Two husbands wished that their wives would not end all telephone conversations with a high pitched, 'Bye, bye dear.' One wife disliked her husband's habit of, in her opinion, blinking his eyes so much when he was speaking.

Yes, we noted when talking with him he did blink his eyes. It didn't bother us. However, we were with him only 45 minutes, not 45 years.

50

Ingrained Habits

Did you know that some husbands, and a few wives, have the habit of leaving the bathroom door ajar when using the facilities? Or that there are men who persist in leaving their hammer on the kitchen table after completing a minor repair job? (Probably because they have the habit of rewarding themselves with a cup of coffee and then forget their tools.) As one offended wife complained, 'I wouldn't mind if the hammer was there once in a while. But every time?'

We also uncovered a whole category of habits that we refer to as 'verbal habits'. We are all aware that in recent years the young have developed the habit of inserting a 'Ya know' at the end of almost every sentence. But such verbal habits are not restricted to the young. We heard reports of older men and women who over-punctuated their conversation with too many 'Ahs' and 'Ers', and even grunts, to their mate's distraction.

And the habit of not finishing sentences came up surprisingly often. As one wife lamented, 'My husband knows for sure what he is going to say and seems to think I know how he will finish the sentence, so he doesn't finish it.' Please don't laugh. Just make sure that you are a sentence-finisher. There seem to be too few of them about.

The major problem with verbal habits and, in truth, all habits is that the offender is not aware, for the most part, of his or her irritating habits. So, we have a suggestion that we have recommended to various couples, and they have been kind enough to report back that it has been helpful.

The suggestion is this. Tonight, or tomorrow morning, when your married life is on an even keel, ask your wife, or your husband, 'Would you please tell me, dear, what are my two habits that annoy you the most? I can't promise that I will be able to do anything about them, but I will try. And, anyway, I would just like to know what they are. Don't give me your answer now. Think about it, and if you do not want to divulge my two most irritating habits, just tell me two of the less irritating variety.'

With a little bit of luck your spouse will ask you the same question. The result will be, if nothing else, some stimulating conversation; and, we would hope, a little better mutual understanding; and, in time, an even more satisfactory marriage.

12
Marital Encouragement

Don't let it retire when you retire.

Our first real encouragement, and we were not conscious of it, came from our parents when we took our first halting step, alone, those many years ago.

No doubt they heaped such praise on us as, 'That's wonderful, darling' and 'Imagine that! And you are only eleven months old. Amazing!'

From then on our parents continued to encourage us in our school work, our sports, and all our other interests. And for many of us, grandparents lent an important hand in giving us an occasional encouraging lift. Then teachers, especially the fine teachers, gave us encouragement even though at times we may not have deserved it.

Even when we went to work our bosses saw to it that we were encouraged from time to time. With enough encouragement about them, young married couples automatically encouraged each other.

Unfortunately, by the time retirement is reached we no longer have parents, or teachers, or bosses to encourage us. The only people left to give us periodic encouragement is our own husband, or our own wife. And this is at the stage of our lives when we need as much emotional support as we can find.

What concerned many of the couples we interviewed was the fact that months and years would pass without either of them hearing even one genuinely encouraging word.

In a talk with Nancy and Phil K. they said that they had discussed the subject recently together and put their finger on what they considered the problem – and worked out a possible solution.

Here is what they reported. 'Since we have been retired we have made an extra effort to be polite to each other. We try to remember to say "thank you" and "please" and "excuse me" whenever the words are called for. Further, we think we have recognized the need for each of us to remember important anniversaries, like the day we met, or became engaged, and certainly birthdays and wedding anniversaries.

'However, we have been so busy being polite, we have over-looked the need to be encouraging. There's a big, big difference between being polite and being encouraging.'

Other couples asked us what we meant when we asked about their ability to be encouraging. Our reply was to quote what Nancy told us, and later Phil confirmed. Nancy reported, 'I know it sounds silly but when Phil told me last week that he thought I made even better cakes now than I did when we were first married, I was delighted. And while I am not much of a knitter he kept encouraging me for months until I finally finished a little sweater for our granddaughter.'

Phil added, 'Yesterday, we were reviewing our finances and, all of a sudden, Nancy remarked that I must have been very smart to start putting money into a Building Society thirty-five years ago as it now is what keeps us going comfortably. Call it encouragement, call it praise, call it what you will, that buoyed me up. And one day when I happened to break a 100 playing golf, you would have thought from her response I had won the Open!'

The solution Nancy and Phil recommended was to continue to be as polite to each other as possible, but to try to add an icing to the cake in looking for opportunities to encourage each other. They emphasised that it was not easy; but, when achieved, eminently worthwhile.

They recognized that it was highly unlikely they were going to receive much out-and-out encouragement – whether deserved or not – from any other source than themselves. So they now work at encouraging each other.

13
Teasing

With affection – or with a needle?

HERE was one of our most difficult subjects in our interviews. Practically every couple with whom we talked admitted that, from time to time, they teased each other. From an American husband's, 'Wow, that's a sexy outfit,' when the wife appeared in a pair of baggy blue jeans – to a long suffering English wife's, 'Those muddy boots must be very comfortable, dear, since you keep them on in the house.'

Or even a husband's, 'It takes an adept driver to do two hundred pounds worth of damage to a car when it is being driven at two miles an hour. And I am sure that the tree was standing still.'

Call it kidding each other, jesting, ribbing, or teasing – or whatever – most couples have done it all of their married life. But we found that in retirement, when the two are together more, there is both more teasing, and it can be more biting.

Our difficulty was that almost every husband or wife that we talked to individually claimed that their own teasing was light-hearted, basically a jest, and friendly.

BUT.

When we asked for their observations about other couples they knew well, the picture was almost entirely different.

We heard such comments as, 'How does she stand those constant snide remarks he makes?' Or, 'Why does he sit there and take that steady stream of 'funnies' that she puts out? All of them tear him down.'

So, we began to wonder whether we were getting forthright

answers from our respondents – or were they telling us that they thought that their own 'teasing' was a bit of a joke – but perhaps the recipient looked at it in a different light.

Subsequent interviews revealed that rather more often than you might think, both husbands and wives felt that their spouse's 'teasing' was often irritating; probably, as one husband admitted, because it was 'too close to the bone'.

In addition some husbands – and some wives – told us that what upset them was not necessarily the content of the 'teasing' but the fact it was so repetitive. An innocuous comment, 'Where are you going, dear? The North Pole?' when the wife went out enshrouded with a favourite massive woolley scarf, passed unnoticed when said forty years ago. But hearing it a dozen times each intervening year, the humour begins to fade.

Further, in marriage homes where husbands and wives are of different political persuasions – and, while hard to believe, there are some – the temptation to make fun of the mistakes made by the partner's party is just too great not to comment on with a barb.

One couple in their eighties – and married for over fifty years – told us this story. The husband was an ardent Conservative – the wife a life-long member of Labour. They claimed they had enjoyed a most satisfactory marriage for all these years in spite of their political differences – but they admitted that life was rather tense when there was a general election.

Teasing

When the husband had just retired and they were, of course, together a great deal, he reported that for at least a six month period their relationship was strained because the wife could not resist, as the details of a certain story appeared each morning in the paper, teasing him with, 'You certainly are a good judge of a candidate's character,' (after the candidate had been had up for some sexual indiscretion). Or 'Read this. You'll be delighted with this juicy revelation.' And so on.

Fortunately they survived the period – and even survived his pointed comments to her during the last Labour administration.

Having mentioned the problems which stem from slightly amusing remarks between couples, we want to make sure that we do not discourage friendly 'teasing' between partners. If nothing more it is evidence that one partner recognizes the existence of the other – which in the best of marriages happens all too seldom.

It also maintains some light-heartedness in a marriage – which we encourage with enthusiasm.

However, the 'teaser' must be sensitive to the fact that his or her comments might be taken in a somewhat different light than they are meant. And also there is the ever-present problem that the subject matter of the teasing might be overworked – especially as there is now the opportunity of using it more often.

A PS FROM PHOEBE

After my husband Ted retired and he was always home when I went off to the hairdressers' – and returned with my coiffure in, I thought, very good order – Ted's comment for several years was, with a smile, 'I thought you said you were going to the hairdressers' today.'

Fortunately even Ted agrees that this tease has run its course. Now he makes no comment whatsoever about my rejuvenated hair-do. Frankly, I do not know whether I prefer the tired gag – or the lack of notice. Maybe in a few more years he can bring himself to observe, 'Phoebe, you certainly look good.'

I hope so.

14
Jealousy and Envy

The reasons change, but they still exist.

In the early days of marriage, jealousy, when it raised its ugly head, usually was concerned with another man, or another woman, appearing on the scene.

While we are sure that the same might hold true in an occasional retirement marriage, we found little evidence of it. However, we certainly did discover that many wives and many husbands used the words, 'I am jealous of . . .' in referring to their spouse for a wide variety of other reasons.

In the end we concluded that when they said they were jealous, what they really meant was they were envious. For example, Marian S. told us, 'I'm jealous of Jack. Here he is two years older than I am and he walks four or five miles a day; and with my hip I'm hobbling around on a cane like an old lady.'

And the-other-side-of-the-coin comment that we heard often was best expressed by Harold M. who said, 'Yes, I'm jealous of Mary. Here we are almost exactly the same age (74) and I look ninety, and everybody is always telling her she looks fifty. What little hair I have is grey and hers has scarcely changed – albeit it with a little help from time to time. I'm sick and tired of all our friends telling her how young she looks. I'm glad that she does, but it is still irritating.'

It is easy to say that Harold should be pleased with having a young looking wife. And we sensed that he truly was – although he said later that he would hit the next friend who told him, 'Boy, you've got a beautiful daughter.' In his opinion, this joke had worn out.

Anther form of jealousy, or envy, affected both husbands and wives who had mates who were exceedingly popular, while they were more on the reserved side. Ruth F. admitted, 'We belong to a little club and every time we go there Bill is the centre of attraction. He talks with everybody. People come up to him all of the time; while my role is to sit and listen. Since he has retired he seems to have become even more popular.' Then she added wistfully, 'And I have become less.'

But we had almost an equal number of husbands who were jealous, they said, of their wife's ability with small talk. At gatherings of any kind these wives could meet some one they had never seen before and within seconds be deep in an animated conversation, while the husband was shifting from foot to foot emitting unintelligible mumbles.

We found wives who were jealous of their husband's ability to cook better than they did; and we found retired husbands who were a bit jealous of their wives' athletic ability. They might be smiling, but to be beaten by your wife every time you play tennis or golf or bowls still hurts. (Incidentally, we were amazed to find in how many marriages the wife does have more athletic ability than her husband. Part of the reason may be that husbands tend to be older than their wives, so the latter still have more youth on their side.)

One positive facet of the jealousy/envy problem is that practically all of our respondents who raised the question admitted that the source of their envy had been around long before retirement and that, by now, they had learned, more or less, to live with it.

The major, and very important, exception is in the area of health when one member has remained in much better physical shape than the partner.

We wish we had been able to come up with a 100% certain solution to this situation, but we have not. After middle age few people change radically from being shy and reserved to becoming a centre of attraction; from being a stumbling conversationalist to having an agile tongue; or from having limited athletic ability to becoming club champion.

We do recommend that you do your best to turn your envy

into admiration for those assets at which your mate excels. After hours of conversation on this subject we are convinced that in every couple with whom we talked both parties had assets of which the other could be a little, or a lot, jealous.

So rather than expending energy being envious, it is better to appreciate your own assets, and admire your partner's.

And don't tell Harold that you think his wife looks young enough to be his daughter.

15
Bones of Contention

Why a write-out is better than a shoot-out.

We will talk about quarrels (Topic 31). But there is another aspect of marital discord which comes into a rather different category. Not always, but sometimes.

The flare-ups are one thing; and even the sulking, which goes on much longer, has a limited lifespan. But there are also the long-standing bones of contention which never quite get resolved. At intervals, they may lead to the flare-ups and the sulking; and long-term this is not much help to a marriage. Like the common cold, they keep coming back.

After discussing this subject with many of our interviewees, we feel there is much to be said for sitting down at a very clear-headed moment in the day – like eleven in the morning – and actually writing down your point of view. Explaining exactly why you, the husband or the wife, feel you have a case to be answered.

This is *not* an easy option. Some people are not very fluent on paper; and even if they are, the effort of marshalling their thoughts in cold blood, and making their 'case' as convincingly as possible, is hard work. It is easier, and perhaps more immediately satisfying, to have yet another verbal shoot-out with your spouse.

But the 'write-out', as an alternative, does have advantages. The fact that it makes you think in a reasonably unemotional and logical way is one of them.

Quarrels and arguments between husbands and wives usually throw up any number of accusations, counter-accusations, and tired old phrases. The fact that you have been married a long time makes the 'tired' aspect more probable.

Iris P. wrote, 'I'm afraid it's a bit like putting on a scratchy old record. You've heard it all before. You know you'll hear it again. And although you get very excited and angry, I sometimes think that Paul and I don't really *listen* to each other. In some ways, it's just too boring.'

However, if you write down your point of view on paper, you can take a conscious decision *not* to use any of the familiar phrases. ('You never consider what I want' or 'You're always rude to *my* friends' or 'You're just so selfish' or 'Just so lazy' etc and etc.)

In the heat of the moment these phrases can be hard to avoid, and once spoken cannot be unspoken. Written phrases, on the other hand, can always be deleted or revised. That's a big plus.

You can aim to say something different; or, at least, say it in a different way. This makes more impact. You can also make an effort to see things from your partner's point of view; also, perhaps, include some nice things which never come readily to mind when you are shouting at each other. Another big plus.

One correspondent, Lionel D., made the effort to sum up some rules. He did remarkably well. He said that he and his wife had tried the 'write-out' solution a few years after he retired. 'I don't know why we'd never tried it before, but I suppose we were both busy and felt we didn't have the time for such an exercise.'

But now the exercise had proved to be a great success and Lionel was able to recommend it whole-heartedly . . . . 'Particularly,' he added, 'for couples like Maureen and myself who are now spending so much more of our lives together and need to get some old arguments sorted out.'

Lionel's rules are simple:

1. Give your write-out time. Time to think. Time to revise.
2. DON'T repeat yourself.
3. Include a few surprises.
4. Include some love.
5. Keep it as short as possible.
6. Don't do it too often.

As we have warned you the 'write-out' can be something like very hard work. Perhaps, Lionel's last piece of advice is the best of all.

16
Marital Deafness

Your marriage doesn't suffer from it?
You're one in a million.

IN our topic 'HOUSE RULES' you will find that many of the recommended rules were concerned with the problem that long-married couples have in just simple communication with each other. 'Don't talk to me when I am out of the room!' and, 'Don't ask me to do something unless I'm looking into your eyes!' were typical of the complaints.

When we pursued this topic in personal interviews we usually opened up a very sensitive subject. In most cases it was the wife who lamented, 'I tell him something and later he swears that if I did tell him, he didn't hear me.'

Stop! Before you make a judgement on this subject it would be well to hear the male side of the story. Their report contained such statements as, 'When we are sitting quietly reading a book, or watching TV, and I start to leave the room for some reason, as soon as I am beyond the limits of easy earshot, she says something to me. It seems that there is a device in the door jamb that triggers, for example, a request like, "When you come back please bring me the morning paper." So when I return from the loo two minutes later, and without the paper, I get a lecture about not listening properly.'

Many other husbands said in essence that while they are watching on TV the last few minutes of a football match, and their favourite team has the ball in the opponent's penalty area, the wife will say, 'Don't forget to call Charlie tomorrow and tell him we can't get there until 6pm.' Two days later when you are leaving for Charlie's she will ask, 'Did you call him and tell him we would be late?' the answer is invariably 'No!'

The question then becomes, 'Did he forget? Or was he never properly told?'

We do not know the correct answer – and no amount of discussion with the two partners will uncover a unanimous decision. Harry S., an avid reader, told us that he has finally convinced his wife after thirty-seven years he will not be responsible for any requests made while he has his reading glasses on.

Harry claimed that, over the years, when he was deep in a book, he had developed the ability to respond to a comment from his wife with an automatic 'Yes, dear' and never hear a word. He told us their recent agreement concerning his reading glasses works quite well. Now his wife starts by saying, 'Harry, please take off your reading glasses.' And after a moment, 'Would you put the lawnmower in the garage? It's starting to rain.'

Other couples have solved the problem by agreeing not to say anything that has to be remembered before 10am – while others have the same arrangement for the evenings.

On one point we did find agreement – and that had to do with shouting, or more delicately, 'raising your voice'. For some reason when a person shouts, the partner at whom the shout is directed, hears the shout all right, but is so absorbed by it that he, or she, often forgets the content of the request.

We had sad stories from several husbands who admitted that when they were supposed to have heard a statement from their wives they often guessed at what she had said to avoid asking her to repeat it. Mark N. thought his wife had asked him, as he was departing one morning to the supermarket, to buy 'some eggs and bacon'. A quite logical request. He duly bought them only to find she wanted eggs and baking powder – the latter for a cake for a WI sale that afternoon.

Our strong recommendation. Don't guess! If you do not have the full message take the risk of asking for a repeat.

A communication problem reported by many more wives than husbands concerned one of the partners not giving full details when discussing a subject. Betty H. told a typical story, 'Yesterday when I was out my good friend telephoned. Bill took the message. When I returned home and asked what she had said, all I got was that her cold was better but that their dog was sick. He forgot to mention that her twenty-nine year old daughter had become engaged and they were planning a wedding in March.'

One final communication irritant we found was the tendency of some women and men always to use the words, 'I've already told you . . . .' when asked about some subject on which the questioner should be knowledgeable. The answer to the query, 'When are we due at the Jones's?' all too often gets an answer, '*I've already told you*, six o'clock.'

Of course, you probably have already told him or her, but, as with shouting, the technique dominates the message – and you may have to repeat the information yet again. It is a hard habit to break, particularly – as right is usually on the speaker's side.

However, the words, 'I've already told you' have an impact on the recipient roughly the same as 'You dumb-bell'. And this surely does not encourage marital harmony.

Unfortunately, we have no suggested answer to the problem of 'marital deafness'. We believe it is a problem, occasionally serious, in nearly all marriages.

All that we can recommend is for you both to be aware that there are many pitfalls when two people try to communicate and the more sensitive you are of your partner's shortcomings, the better it will be for both.

There has been no hearing aid invented that will absolutely cure every case of marital deafness. The problem is that the affliction usually has nothing to do with the mechanism of the ear – but rather with the penetration of the brain.

★ ★ ★ ★

A RURAL REPORT

'Women are queer cattle. By the time you retire, the better you know how to handle queer cattle.'

A Yorkshire farmer

★ ★ ★ ★

17
Holidays

Do you ever take one? Alone?

ON one of our very earliest interviews, a Ted K. told us bluntly, 'Since I retired the only thing that keeps our marriage together is the fact that we take occasional separate holidays. And please understand that we think we have a damned good marriage; but we do believe in having a few weeks apart each year.'

You can't be much clearer than that.

However, as we talked with more and more couples we found the completely opposite view stated just as bluntly. As Nancy B. said, 'I just can't imagine going on any kind of a holiday without Jack. I wouldn't enjoy it, and I'm sure he wouldn't either. Furthermore, I would think separate holidays would weaken any marriage.'

The more we discussed this the more we found that there was no grey area. Either you favoured the idea, or you disliked it intensely.

Among those that thought separate holidays were a good idea were Milton and Betty M. He loved to travel. She disliked it intensely. He loved visiting museums. On this she was indifferent. She preferred working in her small garden. So twice a year Milton took himself off to the Continent for a week – stayed in small hotels – went to six or seven new museums. While Betty had a week in which she did not have to worry about meals for anyone but herself and she could really have time to get the whole garden in good shape.

We found men who had an avid interest in photography who

would go off for short periods on their own to take pictures while their wives pursued their own hobbies nearer home. Several wives were ardent bird-watchers – and their husbands were not. As Joan L. said, 'If I suggested to Al that he had to sit with me in a hide in the middle of a muddy marsh for three hours to spot a golden plover, he'd rebel.'

While we did find a marked difference of opinion as to separate holidays, we found that most of the couples that favoured them consisted of one member with a hobby or interest not shared to the same degree by the partner. However, there were couples who just thought it was a good idea to be apart for a period each year. One or the other said they just planned to go off for several days, or several weeks, once or twice a year to stay with a friend or relative – not to do anything in particular.

Without exception those that believed in an occasional separate holiday reported that after these breaks they seemed to enjoy their partners more, and appreciate them more – especially the husbands who had had to cope with the household chores while their wives had been away.

In discussing separate holidays we were interested to find many couples where one member had taken up a new interest or hobby just so the two could take holidays together. Kevin S. even took up bird-watching. He confessed, 'I always thought Mildred's interest in bird-watching was ridiculous. And when I was working I was pleased for her to go off for long weekends with her binoculars. I was busy at work. But when I retired I agreed to give it a try and found that I enjoyed it. Now we go off together.'

Some wives learned how to play an acceptable game of golf or tennis after retirement just in order to share a husband's holiday – and the latter always seemed to be pleased by this.

We concluded that by the time retirement arrived most couples had long since agreed upon a family policy on this subject. They accepted that separate holidays were either a very good idea – or a very bad one. We found few couples where one member felt strongly that a period apart each year would help their marriage, while the other member disagreed. This is indeed fortunate as it certainly is an important marriage matter – in retirement or before.

However, we found men and women asking us what we thought about separate holidays in the light of our many conversations with fellow retirees. Before giving our answer, we should tell you that both of us enjoy marriages where we do take an occasional separate holiday. It is not a 'must' and we don't plan them; but when something comes up of interest to one member, and not the other, we think it is a good idea to go off on our own. It adds a new interest for a considerable period after we are back together again.

So we are a bit prejudiced. We can make a good case for having a separate holiday. Basically we would recommend that all retirement couples should, at least, consider them. On the other hand we are very sensitive to the arguments put forward by the non-separate-holiday believers, and if both members feel strongly on the subject, after talking it over, we do not think they should change their opinion this late in life.

We do think that all couples should sit down of a quiet evening and ask each other, 'How do we feel about an occasional separate holiday?' And, 'Do you think we should consider one as a sort of an experiment?'

You'll come up with the right answer for your marriage.

18
Cheerfulness

Where do you fit on a scale of 1 to 10?

AFTER our interviews we tried to evaluate the cheerfulness quotient of each husband, each wife, and the couple together. Then we gave everyone a 'cheerfulness rating'. A 10 rating would be for someone wildly cheerful – a 1 rating would go to someone extremely dour.

At the same time we took into consideration the following:

A. Health. A person who was quite cheerful though crippled with arthritis would get a somewhat higher rating than someone without such a handicap.

B. Finances. Similarly, a couple with a very limited income who seemed not to be downcast and discouraged, and still cheerful, would rate higher than a couple very well off.

C. Family problems. If we uncovered serious family problems – primarily problems connected with children and grandchildren – we took into consideration how they were coped with them in awarding the cheerfulness rating.

We cannot claim that our research was definitive. There were too many subjective judgements involved. However, we are confident that we can claim that in those instances where we judged the cheerfulness rating to be above average – 7's and 8's and even a few 9's – we found long term marriages that we thought were significantly happier than where the rating was a 2 or a 3.

We, of course, found cheerful husbands (an 8) with a wife whom we thought was a 3; and we found quite a few wives (to whom we gave 9's) married to 2's and 3's. All in all we found the cheerfulness rating in wives somewhat higher than in the average husband. (You could speculate and draw all kinds of conclusions from this, but we did not think it possible to determine accurately why this should be so.)

We awarded very few 10's – and no single couple received more than an 8. (We are certain that if there were two 10's in the same family, their marriage would be so aggressively cheerful that it would be as bad as if, on the other end of the scale, two 1's lived together. In the latter case the marriage would be showing a very grim face to the world, but that might not be worse than being nauseatingly cheerful.)

Cheerfulness

It is generally recognized that the ability to be cheerful through thick and thin is a trait you are born with. We agree. It is extremely difficult to learn how to be cheerful if it is not in your nature.

However, if after being married twenty, or thirty, or forty, or more, years you can make yourself at least recognize the importance of cheerfulness in a marriage, even though you may have limited scope in increasing your own level, you will be able to make an important contribution to your own marriage.

Here is a simple exercise that might help. Sit down for a minute and give yourself – *not* your spouse, but yourself – what you think is your own cheerfulness rating. Then, for example, if you give yourself a 3, make a decision to see if you can push it up to a 4 next year.

Or if you give yourself a 5 rating, determine to make it a 6 twelve months from now.

Do not aspire to make yourself an 8 or a 9. It is just not in human nature for a person to change that much. If you can push your rating up just one point over a period of time, you will have made a major contribution to your marriage – and to your whole outlook on life.

Further, we suggest that you do not tell your spouse about your determination to move from a 3 to a 4 – or from 5 to 6. He, or she, will notice the change in due course.

And will appreciate it.

A PS FROM JOE

One day I happened to see Ted, Phoebe's husband, out working in his garden. I walked up to him and, out of the blue, asked him what he thought was the most important ingredient in a retirement marriage.

Without a moment's hesitation – he didn't even look up, his hands were full of recently removed weeds – he answered, 'Cheerfulness.'

19
Looking Back

Interesting? Necessary? Or just self-indulgent?

A mutual American friend of ours, Thelma Walker, told us this story:

My parents were always very kind to various odd relatives. We used to have an old, old uncle for lunch most Sundays. But all he ever did was to talk about things he remembered from . . . . well, to me it seemed a hundred years back. And it wasn't interesting.

At the time I was thirteen and reading quite a bit. One lunch this uncle had been remembering more than usual. Somehow I got a word in edgeways, and said to my father, 'You know what Montaigne wrote? He said when you start to look back, you start to die.'

Oh me. Did things ever go quiet? I can remember, as if it was yesterday, my father's face as he said, 'Shush!' And I guess he changed the subject.

Looking forward is normal for the young. Sixty years later looking back can be equally normal. And if no one looked back on their lives history would be a very impoverished affair. Most of us have enjoyed reading autobiographies. To many it is a favourite form of reading.

But in terms of conversation between husband and wife, endless reminiscing, on either side, can be a mistake; even on a par with repeating the same stories. It is an easy habit to get into because this kind of conversation requires little effort. Thelma's uncle, maundering on about the past, hardly had to think at all. It was like turning on a tap; he never stopped to ask himself if what came out was of any interest to his hearers.

Some reminiscing can be fun. Particularly a long-married couple reminiscing together. As Edna C. reminded us. 'Tim and I still laugh when we think of my grandmother's funeral. She loved roses. I asked Tim to order a wreath of roses with a card from us. Well, the wreath was fine, but Tim didn't bother to look at the card. He just picked one out with roses on it. Inside it said, 'HAPPY BIRTHDAY, MOM, AND MAY YOUR NEXT FIFTY YEARS BE JUST AS ROSY.'

That kind of concentration on the past is fine. And is another subject entirely. Our concern is with the dangers pointed out by one of our correspondents, George G., who thinks that always living in the past makes you a dull person to live with.

George thinks it is all right to do it now and again but not on a regular basis. 'I don't care how old you are. Unless you keep looking forward to SOMETHING, you get to be a depressing person to have around the house. Your mate begins to think there's nothing to look forward to either, and you end up a couple of gloomsters.

'I'm not saying you rule out the past. It's part of life and there are lots of things one likes to remember. Just don't live with it. Always keep one eye looking ahead.'

(We discovered, incidentally, that George was coming up to his ninetieth birthday.)

We concluded that when it comes to looking back an important word was 'sharing' as opposed to just 'telling'. Sharing implies that you are thinking about the person or persons at the receiving end; will this interest, stimulate, amuse THEM? Will they come back with memories or comments that will do the same to you?

Telling, on the other hand, is one-sided. The reminiscer is unlikely to ask himself if the audience wants to hear any of it.

It is hard to believe that any one would want to wake up in the morning and find that they could remember nothing of their past life. The ability to look back can reasonably be described as necessary.

It can also be interesting to other people; and particularly to a wife or husband who has shared some or all of it. The self-indulgence only arises when the looking back becomes repetitive, obsessive, one-sided.

That's when we should remember a song from a famous English musical:

> If I once start looking behind me,
>   And begin retracing my track,
> I'll remind you to remind me,
>   We said we wouldn't look back.

20
House Rules

Do any of these apply to your house?

WE sent a hundred retired couples a questionnaire in which we asked, among other questions, each husband and each wife to give us three house rules that they wished could be made to stick in their own house.

We expected to receive 300 house rules from women and 300 more from their husbands. But that did not happen. Once they started to think up house rules they would like, they could not stop at three – some suggested ten rules – and we ended up with over a thousand.

There were some subjects on which quite a few contributed. The most popular area was this one:

IT SHOULD BE
A HOUSE RULE

. . that we don't try to talk to each other unless we're in the same room.

or

. . that my wife doesn't start to talk to me unless she is close enough to touch me.

and

. . that you don't talk to me when I am in the bathroom.

and

. . that if he needs a hearing aid even a little bit he should wear it.

Family communication was the number one subject. Close behind was dust and dirt. Mostly contributed by husbands. Here are some examples:

. . that if you can't notice the dirt from across the room, don't clean it.
also
. . that the house does not have to be cleaned as often as a wife thinks.
and
. . that wives shouldn't take housework too seriously and thereby miss spur-of-the moment chances to do something together. The dust will keep.

However, we were surprised to find that the suggested house rules covered literally hundreds of different subjects. Here are some of them:

. . that husbands should let wives finish a story.
. . that it is understood that nothing is as important as a little sloping-off time – like a game of backgammon in mid-morning with a second cup of coffee.
. . that neither partner worries about little things.
. . that nothing, but nothing, is kept from your spouse.
. . (obviously from a husband) that you tell me how much you spent *now*. Don't wait for me to discover it.

. . that there is no serious conversation until after my second cup of coffee.

. . that no one start a serious conversation when I'm watching a serious TV show.

. . that my husband let me answer all questions directed to me.

. . (from a wife) that now you have mastered the dishwasher you should learn to give the washing machine a whirl.

. . that wives go easy on the curry powder.

. . that husbands always put the toilet seat down.

. . that retired couples should look at the world with the wonder of children.

. . that a husband has to throw out his share of the past forty years – and don't spare the horses.

. . that a wife does not always imagine the worst.

. . that all telephone calls should be limited to five minutes.

. . that wives understand husband's devotion to TV sports.

And these are just a sampling of the suggested house rules.

Finally, we are indebted to one of our respondents for the following house rule which made us stop and think. It should be, in our opinion, a house rule with every marriage.

IT SHOULD BE A HOUSE RULE that you treat your partner like a friend. This requires more consideration and courtesy than is usually accorded a spouse.

However, we cannot end this report on house rules without expressing our thanks to two other respondents who suggested:

IT SHOULD BE A HOUSE RULE that there are *no* house rules.

Do you agree?

★ ★ ★ ★

EATING YOUR HEART OUT

It's ground for divorce when a retired husband wants potatoes twice a day.

Maria Jay

★ ★ ★ ★

21
Criticism

A pat on the back, before a kick in the pants.

We never anticipated the amount of discussion we would engender when we first asked the men and women we interviewed the question, 'Are you very critical of your spouse – and vice-versa?'

Almost half of our respondents said that criticism by their partner was a more important problem than it was before retirement. Mona D. explained, 'Paul's occasional critical remarks about me did not bother me unduly when we were together so few hours every week. But now that we are together so many more hours I find I am being criticized about five times as much as before – and I know the only reason is that we see each other about five times more each week than we used to.'

By the time retirement comes around almost all husbands and wives are used to their mate's tendency to be critical; and they have, more or less, learned to live with it. However, when criticism increases four or five fold, merely because you are together more often, it causes much marital irritation. We were surprised how much.

When we talked privately with both husbands and wives who admitted that they might be over critical of their partner, we often received an answer like, 'Until you mentioned the subject I never gave this unfortunate habit of mine much thought.'

In other words they considered this habit to be of no consequence. As one husband admitted, 'I never thought it was more important than my habit of pulling on my right ear lobe when I am talking.' And he continued, 'Now that I think about it I'll try to be less critical in the future. Pulling on an ear lobe does not bother my wife, but I'm sure my habit of being critical does.'

He was so right, as his wife confided to us later.

There is not much more we can say about marital criticism than that it is an irritating habit, and should be kept at an absolute minimum.

One way of accomplishing this is to make a mental note of how many times a day you say something pleasant, something positive, something encouraging to your spouse. And then be critical a few less times than that total. Men and women who have tried this solution tell us that they worked so hard in being non-critical that they soon lost the habit of being over critical. And their world was better for it.

One top business executive, well known for his ability to stimulate the people that worked for him, told us that he had a firm personnel relationship theory. It was simply:

A PAT ON THE BACK, BEFORE A KICK IN THE PANTS.

In his aggressive business atmosphere it was necessary for him from time to time to be highly critical of an employee. However, before he ever mentioned his criticism he always found something about the employee which he could genuinely praise *before* expressing his criticism.

In business one pat on the back helps soften one critical observation.

In a retirement marriage we suggest, two pats on the back for each critical kick in the pants.

Maybe three.

★ ★ ★ ★

ATOMIC CONCLUSIONS

Soon after I retired my wife said to me, 'Why don't we spend this morning sitting in the sun together?' And, you know, it was one of the happiest afternoons of my life.

A nuclear scientist

★ ★ ★ ★

22
Behaviour in Public

Public praise, public criticism, public manners.

Two years after he retired, Michael W. found he was missing something. It wasn't anything obvious like a regular job or friends at work. In fact he was half embarrassed to tell us the truth.

'It sounds childish,' he said, 'but I missed people saying nice things about me – and particularly in public. This happens on a job. Not all of the time, of course, but sometimes. Then you retire and suddenly there's only your wife to pay any compliments.'

It seemed that Michael's wife kept her compliments, especially public compliments, in short supply. She was kind and affectionate in private, but . . . 'When we're out with friends she says things like "Mike's not handy around the house. He has trouble replacing a light bulb; or, Mike's had those trousers for twenty years." Always little barbs rather than praise.'

Not two days later, Mabel F. confessed to us, 'I don't understand. When we're alone Jack often tells me I look nice, or that the meal was pleasing to him – praise which really makes my day. But in public, or even with the children around, he never comes out with anything remotely like a compliment. Why?'

We began to find that the whole question of behaviour in public was more of a problem than we – and perhaps many others – had recognized. And (again!) it was one which provoked different reactions in husbands and wives.

Many husbands, like Michael W., frankly missed the public bouquets which came their way in a job. It was agreed that they didn't have to be big bouquets. No more, perhaps, than a warm 'well done' from a boss; or the comment, 'Wish I could think of an idea like your's,' from a fellow worker.

A retired garage mechanic told us there were times he really craved to hear a customer say, as they had sometimes done after he fixed an engine, 'That's wonderful. It sounds perfect.'

Wives were less concerned with the loss of compliments which came with the loss of a job. (Perhaps jobs were less important to them. Indeed, they may never have had a job at all.) However, they were very concerned with ALL aspects of behaviour in public. Compliments certainly came into it, and Mabel F. was not alone in her complaint, 'Why does he never say anything nice about me in public?'

Above all, wives wanted the world to see them as a happily married couple; and a little public praise now and then would help establish this picture.

A 64-year-old wife sent us a poem:

TO MY DEAR, DARLING, BUT OFTEN CRITICAL, HUSBAND

> Tell me I'm lazy,
> Tell me I'm crazy,
>   Tell me I look like a witch:
> Tell me each meal
> Is a miserable deal,
>   Tell me I act like a bitch.
>
> Mumble and mumble,
> Grumble and grumble,
>   End every word with a groan:
> My love will survive
> If you can contrive
>   To do it when we are ALONE!
>
> But do it all in front of friends
> And that's the way the loving ends.

Most husbands like to have their egos bolstered in public, but they worry far less about the general appearance of a marriage.

We don't think they would sympathize with Joan O.'s comment. 'My husband is just too damn casual in public, as if I didn't count for anything special in his life. We still have a happy marriage after forty years, and I know that's what really counts. But I still feel he could take more trouble when we are out together. At any time of life you want the world to know that you do love each other.'

As they grow older men tend to think that their partners are making a fuss about nothing. (We were told that this is particularly true of Englishmen.) Small courtesies, small attentions and compliments in public . . . . do they really matter? After so many years of marriage is it really necessary to worry about the world's view of your marriage?

That's a big point of disagreement.

On the other hand, both husbands and wives agree that the lovey-dovey act in public can be overdone; it can even indicate that there is something wrong with a marriage.

A 60-year-old wife surprised us with the frank statement, 'I knew George was toying with the idea of an affair with another woman when he started being terribly nice to me in public.' (She reassured us that it turned out not to be serious. He was soon back treating her 'more normally' and she knew then he had dropped the idea.)

Another husband wrote, 'It puts me in mind of children who behave like saints outside the home, and are devils to their parents inside. We've all come across them, haven't we? Just as we've all come across couples who were too good to be true in public – and the next thing you know, they're separated.'

There is also agreement about quarrels in public. Not just minor arguments or good-tempered bickering, but ugly stand-up rows which imply a real rift in the relationship.

As we stress in our topic on QUARRELS, these rows can happen late, as well as early, in marriage. But older couples feel strongly – more strongly than the young – that they should happen in private. The old adage, 'Don't wash your dirty linen in public' was very much accepted by our correspondents, though some admitted that they didn't always avoid it.

But we must come back to the point of difference, not

agreement, because this is where change is needed. And we are about to say something you might consider unusual. Which is, '*don't, don't* talk it over together.'

Conventional wisdom, including ours, decrees that couples should iron out most problems with a long, quiet, reasonable discussion. But there are a few problems which do not respond very well to such treatment – and we believe that this is one of them.

We believe that most husbands are, like Michael W., embarrased by their desire for public compliments. They don't know how to explain the need to their wives – not without sounding conceited or childish. (Many said it was easier with strangers, like us.)

As one husband put it, 'How can you turn to a wife and say, "Please build me up in public, don't knock me down". She wouldn't understand that the building-up happened while I was working and I still need it.'

Ironically, we found that the same husbands failed to understand the importance wives attach to public appearances. The man wants 'building up' in front of the world; but he'll still say that, after so many years together, it does not matter what the world thinks of their marriage.

Neither partner seems able to ask themselves the simple question, 'If I want him/her to be nice to me in public, shouldn't I set an example?'

SO, BOTH OF YOU. PLEASE LISTEN TO US AND, MORE IMPORTANT, LISTEN TO ALL THE PEOPLE WHO HAVE TALKED TO US.

Wives really must understand that a retired man is vulnerable. He's missing the encouraging boss, the appreciative colleagues. He needs bolstering in public as well as in private – and *you* are now the person to do it. This is not silly or childish – it's natural.

Husbands must stop thinking just of themselves. If the public appearance of a marriage matters more to a woman than to a man, *indulge her*. You want her to bolster your ego. Shouldn't you also be concerned about bolstering hers?

The small courtesies, attentions we mentioned earlier comes into this and should never be forgotten. Take another look at

Joan O.'s contribution and ask yourself, 'Could this apply to me and my wife?' This time be sympathetic.

Both of you should try to avoid hurtful criticism in front of friends. The wife should stop dwelling on her husband's deficiencies as a handy man, or on the age of his clothes.

A husband should never observe that his mate acts like a bitch, still less, looks like a witch.

Both of you must also accept that behavior in public matters. Some wives think it matters even more in later years than it did early on.

THEY COULD BE RIGHT.

A PS FROM PHOEBE

Hurtful criticism in public is one thing. Friendly differences of opinion between marriage partners are another – and these can be fun.

Some of you may remember a radio programme of yesteryear, 'We Beg to Differ'. Questions, mostly light-hearted, were sent in and answered by a panel of experts. That is to say, experts in humour.

They didn't necessarily agree on the answers, and the 'differing' was, as a rule, between the sexes. The star performers were actor and actress, John Clements and Kay Hammond. (Also husband and wife.)

I remember the question, 'Why do women like weddings and funerals better than men?'

Kay Hammond observed the reason was that women had kinder natures and were more willing to share both in happiness and sorrow.

John Clements shot back, 'Women like both weddings and funerals for one reason – and one reason only. They like to see a good man go down.'

No one laughed more than his wife.

23

Talk, Talk, Talk, Talk, Talk.

Or – are you listening?

Every couple we interviewed had comments to make about talk, and talking.

We had forthright complaints from some husbands and some wives who thought that their spouses talked too much – and other complaints that their spouses talked too little. But everyone had something to say about the quantity, and quality, of talk.

It's a subject everyone wants to talk about.

However, before we report on some of our findings we have to say that, not surprisingly, the two of us found ourselves in some rather major disagreement on this subject. It is the old story of the male and female outlook being different. So, as with several other of our topics, we have each put down our own thoughts and stated our opinions individually.

Later, we do have some observations that might be helpful to those couples who have that occasional disagreement about talk.

This time Joe will go first.

All my fellow males will be glad to know that I did get Phoebe to agree that, by and large, women talk more than men. No argument here. Further, most men agreed that there is nothing wrong with that – as long as the amount of female talk is within reason.

I was not surprised to learn – and I do not think that Phoebe was either – that quite a few husbands think that their wives talk too much – some much too much. (And I must confess that even a few wives had complaints about their husbands on this score.)

But what did surprise me was that in almost every case where a husband expressed an opinion – to us, in private – that his wife was, to be polite, excessively vocal, the wife made no bones about the fact that she did not think she could be classed as one of those women 'who talk too much'.

I am convinced that most men and women who err on the side of talking too much deny that they do. They are just not aware of it. For example, one husband told us that recently he kept a stop-watch in his pocket when he and his wife were dining with another couple. He unobtrusively started the watch every time his wife started to talk, and stopped it when any of the others were participating in the conversation.

What was the result?

He found that his wife had been talking a little over 70% of the time – leaving roughly 30% of the conversation for the other three participants. Quite an imbalance.

This man, and we will not even give you his first name so that he can remain anonymous, was enough of a gentleman never to tell his wife what he had done. However, he told us that when they returned home that night he did mention that he thought that she had talked a little too much.

What did he get for his efforts? An absolute denial. There was no way that she would accept that the evening's conversation had not been relatively equal. He quickly dropped the subject.

Phoebe, it is true that men as well as women are often unaware of the magnitude of some of their habits. But when it comes to talking, I cannot believe a woman can so dominate a conversational situation and not be aware of it.

My male colleagues tell me that they can complain to their wives that they are using too much make-up, and the wife will acknowledge that it could be so. Or tell her she is spending too much money. She won't deny it, although she may have an excuse or two. Or even criticize her for not being able to park a car very well, and she will agree that there is, at least, some truth in your observation.

But, Phoebe, tell me why some women – intelligent on many subjects – absolutely deny, when their husbands bring it up, that they suffer from occasional verbal diarrhoea? And in those cases where the wife does acknowledge it, why is she powerless to change her habits?

I know that I get a biased view when I have a discussion with my male colleagues on this subject; but, to a man, those that have had their wives accuse them of talking too little, or too much, immediately admit to the truth of the accusation.

You could claim that some women's talking is like some men's drinking – occasionally they may overdo it. But, for the most part, this is a bad habit in which some husbands partake only a few days a year. While talking too much is usually a 365-day failing.

Meanwhile, Phoebe, I think we men should start a rumour, and spread it far and wide, that talking too much gives you wrinkles. That should solve the problem.

Now it is your turn Phoebe.

Joe, do you remember the scene in 'My Fair Lady' when Professor Higgins on his rudimentary voice recorder turned up the volume and speeded up the tempo of women's voices? The cackling inferno was recognizably feminine; and some of us wives may have winced as well as laughed. I doubt if the same trick could have been played with male voices.

Women like to talk. And yes, they will often deny, most indignantly, that they talk too much even when the accusation is justified.

Why?

One of the main reasons has a lot to do with the value women attach to talk: a value which, they feel, is not adequately shared or understood by men. (Hence the denials that they overdo it.)

But let me begin, Joe, by stressing that you have made a good point. I am sure that husbands everywhere will agree with you. There will be wives, too, who see what you mean although they may not be ready to say so publicly.

Mind you, the same can be true of men. We all know thundering bores who talk-talk-talk-talk about nothing remotely interesting. But I am being magnanimous. I am assuming no male reader of our book is like that. I am also assuming that most of the wives who are reading these words are still married to men to whom they like to talk, and listen, to.

It is obvious that neither partner wants to be an earache. They probably recognize, too, that the danger of nagging/abusive/ superfluous conversation increases with more togetherness. But like the wives who deny that they EVER talk too much – though secretly suspecting that they do – the problem is not tackled.

How can this be done?

I think men could begin by asking themselves a question. 'Why do women talk so much?' Are there good reasons? According to psychologists the answer is a clear 'yes'.

Women feel that silence is basically unfriendly. A kind of rejection. While I was investigating this subject, one psychologist told me, 'If you walk down the street and see someone you like, you stop and talk. If you see someone you dislike, you pass by in silence. Not talking to people could mean you are a little shy; but it's much more likely to mean dislike, indifference, not wanting to be bothered.'

Men are less concerned about this implication. (And I am not sure they can claim it as a virtue.) Wives feel that, even if they cannot think of anything very brilliant to say, the effort of saying *something* is, in itself, a gesture of goodwill. As another psychologist advised me, 'It's like monkeys grooming each other. They may not do it very well. They may go on too long. But it is still a friendly act.'

I think you'll agree, Joe, that wives really work at these 'gestures of goodwill'. When the going gets sticky at a party, it is usually the hostess who tries to keep the conversation moving. And, truly, this is not because she loves the sound of her own voice. It is because she wants the occasion to be a success. And whoever heard of a party – even a very small one – that was successful *and* silent.

When the guests have gone the husband may say to his wife, 'My God, you rattled on.' But he should give her credit for good intentions, particularly if he himself has not made much of a contribution.

As Salina S. told us – and you were there, Joe – 'My husband sometimes just gives up, damn him – and then tells me I talked too much. I have asked him why we should have guests if we are not going to have conversation. I have even suggested that if we are not both going to talk to our guests, we might as well send the food around to their house in a plastic container.'

Conversation between spouses at home is not, of course, the same as party talk. Joe, you may ask why a husband has to make an effort when he has been married thirty or forty years. Especially during the years when a couple is spending so much time together.

Yes, Joe, you do have to make an effort, for basically the same rule applies. Talking, I repeat, is a sign of liking and interest. Who wants to talk with someone they find boring and unlovable? It does not matter how long you have been married; conversation, like a sexual overture, can still suggest you care. A silence may be peaceful and companionable, but not when it goes on too long. A silence that persists, say, for a few hours indicates that something is wrong. And for twenty-four hours, seriously wrong. I do not believe long periods of silence can ever be interpreted by a wife as a compliment.

There is one other point psychologists make. Talking to someone sympathetic can be a form of therapy. It was found, for instance, that in Australia when families in the outback live on their very isolated farms, the wives could well head for a nervous breakdown when the husband was out all day and she had no one to talk to. Husbands were seriously advised to let their wives talk often on their radio telephone to friends and relations. Just talk.

The men, of course, objected that such calls would be quite expensive and used the argument that the only purpose of a telephone was to get some specific information, or make some arrangement. But they were told in no uncertain terms by psychologists, 'A women needs, really needs, to talk. What about? Well, day-to-day happenings, problems, and so on.' This no doubt sounded like pretty silly stuff to the men, particularly as the calls could go on for quite a while. But the husbands were told if they wanted their wives to be happy and well-adjusted, let them talk.

The psychologist who told me this said, 'Men don't like to accept it, but they, too, need such therapy. Many of them bottle things up, shy away from discussing the things that are really on their mind.' Then. after a few seconds thought, he added, 'This could mean they might soon end up on the psychiatrist's couch.'

NOW, OUR JOINT CONCLUSION

Wives should watch it. One can accept the reasons why they like to talk, and must talk, but we feel that they are, at times, liable to overdo it. They must recognize, too, that nagging talk and complaining talk is hardly ever a useful form of conversation unless they impose a strict time limit on themselves. (Maybe this *is* an occasion where a stop-watch would come in handy.) Don't bottle it up. If you have a grumble, go ahead and grumble. Just don't go on about it too long.

That goes for husbands, too.

Both partners should take time to listen to themselves. Boring talk can damage a marriage, even more than too much, or too little, talk. It is always better to put the brakes on yourself before your partner in desperation mumbles quietly, 'For goodness sake *stop*!'

In the ideal world, we would only speak when we had something of great interest to say. But we agree that this standard in unrealistic. In retirement, when life is often less eventful, it may be extra hard to keep your daily talk on a sparkling level; and it would probably sound artificial if you tried.

The stimulus of surprise will also be rare because, let's face it, long-married couples often know what their mates are going to say before they say it. The main thing is to give and take the warmth, the companionship, implicit in conversation – even banal conversation. Anything sparkling or surprising is a bonus.

Even Joe now feels the therapy point, raised by Phoebe, is especially valid. He admitted, 'If Audrey is ever on the phone talking for a long time, I'll tell myself that the bill would be a whole lot bigger if she had to go to a psychiatrist.'

And in those homes where the husbands pride themselves on

being the strong, silent type, we think that these men should recognize that they can still be strong and, at the same time, be somewhat more liberal with the spoken word.

Wives need conversation more than their husbands think. Do not forget women can look on silence as an indication of unfriendliness. And, as we have mentioned elsewhere, the best marriages are those where the partners consider each other as friends.

So, gentlemen, talk to your friend – your wife.

24
Your Metabolism

. . . and why do many of us get fatter as we get older?

A fascinating experiment was once carried out in an American prison.

A group of prisoners, all volunteers, were fed to excess on all the most sinful foods. They ate as much as they could of butter and cream and doughnuts and spaghetti and fried chicken and chips and chocolate and . . . well, most things a weight-watcher is advised to avoid.

After some weeks, results were assessed. A number of the prisoners had blown up like balloons. Others had hardly gained an ounce.

How come?

The experiment could hardly have been carried out in more controlled circumstances. There were no differences in lifestyle and no differences in diet – they all gorged themselves. But the results were amazingly different. There could be only one explanation. A difference in their metabolism.

Weight problems came up regularly in our discussions with retired couples. (Often aggravated by the fact that one spouse had far less trouble keeping it under control than the other. It's a nagging source of discord because a slim husband tends to ask his bulging wife, 'Why can't you just eat less?' And vice-versa.)

So we undertook to do some research on metabolism and it was immediately obvious that it was *not* just a question of eating less. (Remember the American prisoners.) Some people burn up excess calories. Others store them as fat. And it is all to do with the liveliness, or sluggishness, of our metabolism.

92

Your Metabolism

This is a big subject and as this is a book primarily about marriage in retirement – not health – we will stick to the facts that are most likely to affect older couples.

First, the majority of men, any age, have an advantage. Their metabolism tends to be brisker and they find it easier than women to control their weight. When both husband and wife want to slim, and agree on a diet, almost invariably the husband comes up the winner. He sheds more pounds than his partner, and it is extremely annoying to her because – most possibly – she has adhered to the diet more conscientiously than he.

Our comment to the ladies is 'Blame the Good Lord. That's the way he designed the male and female metabolism.'

Second, everyone's metabolism tends to slow down as we get older. The hugh, indulgent meal which we 'burnt up' in our twenties, settles around our hips and waists in our sixties. Again, 'Blame the Good Lord.' While the advantage still remains with the man, there are enough large masculine paunches around to prove that he is not immune to the slowing down 'age effect' on his metabolic rate.

So, what's to be done? *Starve?*

Certainly not! If the retired husband and wife cannot enjoy good food together, that would be a sad outlook. The bright news is that there are ways to stimulate – one might even say rejuvenate – our metabolism. Of course, commonsense rules about intelligent eating must apply. (Even if your metabolism works well you can no longer over-indulge like those young prisoners.)

But if you can recapture some of that wonderful, carefree feeling of the naturally slim – what a bonus it will be!

Some details of the 'metabolic boost' campaign will be set out in the next two topics. This campaign is geared to people who, in the normal process of ageing, have experienced the usual slow-down in their metabolic rate. But it is not a penetential regime. In fact, you will be happily surprised.

Meanwhile, our advice to both husbands and wives who are tempted to make an overweight partner feel like a self-indulgent slob, is to remember the American prisoners.

Be positive and encourage him or her a) to blame their

metabolism rather than their appetite; and b) to give that sluggish metabolism the boost it evidently needs.

Almost certainly, it would help if the slimmer partner agreed to try the same programme. Whatever your weight, it can do nothing but good.

★ ★ ★ ★

A Superior Prayer

Lord, Thou knowest that I am growing older. I ask that you keep me from getting talkative; and particularly from the fatal habit of thinking I MUST say something on EVERY subject on EVERY occasion. Release me from the craving to try to straighten out everybody's affairs. Keep my mind free from the recital of endless detail and give me wings to get to the point.

I also ask for grace enough to LISTEN to the tales of others' pains. Help me to endure them with patience. But SEAL MY LIPS on my own aches and pains – they are increasing and my love of rehearsing them becomes sweeter as the years go by.

Teach me the glorious lesson that OCCASIONALLY, it is possible, that I MAY be mistaken. Keep me reasonably sweet. I do NOT want to be a Saint. Some of them are SO hard to live with. But a sour old person is one of the crowning works of the Devil.

Make me thoughtful, but not moody. Helpful, but not bossy. And with my vast store of wisdom, it seems a pity not to use it all; but Thou knowest, Lord, that I want a few friends at the end.

Amen

A modern language version of a Mother Superior's prayer written in the 15th century and discovered at Rochester Castle.

★ ★ ★ ★

25
The Booster Programme
– Part One

Foods that get your metabolism on the move.

DIETS come in and out of fashion. Right now diets are very involved with fibre and raw foods. Roughage rules!

From the health point of view there is much to be said for them. One may not be enthusiastic about raw carrots and cabbage and watercress and bran and endless lettuce and even more endless grapefruit. But they are good for you. They lead to clear eyes, glowing skin, beautiful bowels, and boundless energy.

They will also slim you down if you keep to them. However, the same is true of almost any diet *if you keep to it*. There's the problem.

A metabolic diet is not quite in keeping with current trends. The truth is that quantities of fibre do very little to stimulate a sluggish metabolism. Nor do they help with the greatest enemy of any diet – hunger.

If you have tried using bran as an appetite suppressant, presuming that it 'fills you up' and makes you uninterested in a coming meal, you will probably have found that it does not really work.

You can't fool your stomach – or not for long. Fibre passes through the system quite quickly so that any satisfaction is shortlived. Your stomach soon says, 'I want some more.' And as bran is an uninteresting food, you may well start craving for something different.

Protein is another matter. It *does* stimulate the metabolism; and because it is digested more slowly, it keeps you un-hungry

95

for longer. This was the advantage of the High-Protein diets. (Drinking Man's Diet, Dr. Atkins Revolution, etc.) You could eat quite indulgently, feel little hunger, and still lose weight.

These diets are now out of favour because they led to unhealthy excesses. People drank too much, gorged on butter and cream as well as meat and fish. When doctors linked animal fats with heart disease and cancer, there had to be some re-thinking. It also became evident that even if you did not get cancer or have a coronary, excessive amounts of fat and protein made you liverish.

However, it looks as if the swing against proteins has gone too far. If you want to boost your metabolism, you should not try to live without them. At the same time this should be balanced by some favourites from the high fibre diets. Raw fruits and vegetables are needed; though, if you are not a rabbit – as most modern diets assume you are – the amount of raw vegetables need not be excessive.

We suggest the following basic guidelines:

1. Eat little and often. Eating stimulates the metabolism, encouraging it to burn up calories. Caution – this boost disappears if too much food is taken, particularly of the wrong kind.
2. Always eat protein when you feel really hungry. It is the only way to stop the pangs returning swiftly.
3. Raw protein – yes, raw – is an excellent stimulant for your metabolism, and a good appetite suppressant.

Raw protein?

It is a pity that oysters are so expensive, and not to everyone's taste, because nothing could be better. At the end of this topic you will find a recipe for marinating less pricey fish – like cod or haddock. They are *delicious* and truly do not taste in the least raw.

Raw liver is splendid.

Raw liver? UGH!

What could sound more disgusting? However, in spite of the fact that neither of us likes liver, we have discovered a painless method of consumption.

It is this. Thoroughly chill a good quality liver – calves' or lambs'. Cut up two or three ounces into very small, lozenge-shaped pieces. Swallow them whole, like little pills, with some dry red wine. You don't taste the liver at all – only the wine.

This has no pretension to being a gastronomic feast. However, the same could be said for bran tablets. The point is that it is a very effective appetite suppressant – you won't feel hungry for at least two hours – and best of all it is an excellent booster to your metabolism.

4. Sorry – but all the familar baddies: cakes, sweets, chocolates, puddings, almost anything sugary, are not helpful. Once your metabolic rate gets moving a moderate amount can be included. But to begin with they have to be treated as enemies.

5. Alcohol can be a stimulant. A dry wine with a balanced meal will do you nothing but good. And a whisky after a meal can be recommended with a clear conscience.

The bad news is that pre-meal drinks of any kind are dangerous. They sharpen the appetite and make unwise eating more likely. Hard liquor and sweet wines are best avoided – except for one post-meal whisky. These precautions are for the early stages. More indulgence can be allowed once your metabolism is back in high gear.

6. Set aside at least two weeks for this Booster Programme. If you have a long-standing and hefty weight problem, this may have to be extended to four.

If you keep on these guidelines, you can't possibly go hungry. But you will have to keep on them very strictly.

7. Animal fats? What about them?

Do not rule them out entirely. They are needed to keep the joints lubricated. Also, do not let any one tell you that either fat-free or salt-free cooking can be delectable. *It isn't.* On your Booster Programme just don't overdo it.

Good luck to you – and to your metabolism, You will find it will make a considerable difference to your enjoyment of your later years.

OUR FIVE-STAR BOOSTER MEAL – which also happens to be delicious.

½ pound firm white fish.
(Halibut is superb,
but cod or haddock is good.)
Limes or lemons

Onion
Olive Oil
Chopped parsley
Salt and pepper

Remove any bones or skin, and cut the fish into pieces – about 3 inches long, 1 inch wide, and ¼ inch thick. Place in container with tight fitting lid. Cover the pieces of fish with slices of onion; season with salt (preferably sea salt), and add enough lime or lemon juice to cover. Mix up, put on lid and leave in fridge for 12 hours. Shake it occasionally during this period. After 12 hours, turn on to a plate and remove onion. Squeeze juice from the fish. Dribble a little virgin olive oil over the fish, season with pepper and salt and sprinkle with chopped parsley.

Serve on lightly buttered brown toast. (Genuine wholemeal.) A mixed salad is a nice companion. The fish tastes good enough to offer your most discriminating friends. *Not raw at all*. It is also satisfying and healthy – and 'boosting'. What more can you ask?

26
The Booster Programme
– Part Two

What part does exercise play in stimulating your metabolism?

Many of us find it comforting, wickedly comforting, to read about the misfortunes of exercise-addicts. They look marvellous. They never stop telling us how wonderful they feel. And then they do something dreadful to their knees or backs, and even their hearts, while out jogging.

Dr. McCarter of Texas University (of all places), while researching people's lifespans, actually came up with the theory that exercise can *shorten* lives. We lazybones may well achieve a riper old age than all those glowing athletes.

Unfortunately, a challenging theory like Dr. McCarter's is always contradicted by another. It is not such good news to read in another report from America that just three weeks of prone inactivity can result in physical decline equal to thirty years of ageing.

As so often happens, compromise seems to be the best solution. However, not one of the experts we consulted suggested that we can help move our metabolism to a livelier rate by just sitting around all day. Exercise *does* play an important role. Even our own experience confirms that we always feel much better when we keep reasonably active.

Research into metabolic rate has turned up some interesting facts – which may surprise you. It is not so much a question of how much you do in the way of exercise, or how strenuously you do it. It is more of a question of *how often* and, even more important, *when*.

99

Experiments have shown that differences in metabolic rate show up directly after a meal. In other words, a slim person and a fat person will dispose of their calories at more or less the same speed during much of the day. When they are sitting, or walking, or sleeping, or taking more energetic exercise like playing tennis.

The big difference comes after eating. This is when a lively metabolism swings into action, utilizing the calories that are needed by various organs of the body and burning off the excess. On the other hand, a sluggish metabolism utilizes the calories more slowly, and often less efficiently. Moreover, instead of burning off the excess, these calories are stored as (unwanted) fat.

This basic fact explains why so many exercise programmes do not do much for our metabolism and do not, therefore, help us lose weight.

Mistake number one. The working man or woman often feels that the only time of day to 'do exercises' is first thing in the morning, usually before breakfast.

This is understandable because you are in a hurry and what chance do you have to get down on the floor and swing your legs around at your place of work? But as a lifelong habit, extending into the retirement years, it is a mistake.

Come the morning, your metabolism wakes up and operates better than at other times of the day. The boost is needed at other times; and now that working life need not interfere, both husband and wife – as a new aspect of their life together – can start again.

Mistake number two. The thought that the occasional workout, perhaps at an exercise club, is all that is needed.

Your metabolism does not benefit all that much from anything occasional. If it is slowing down, or is already in the doldrums, something more consistent and frequent is needed.

Mistake number three. I must sit down and put my feet up after a meal.

It's tempting; particularly if the meal has been a good one. (And exceptions can always be made.) But do not kid yourself that this siesta is needed for good digestion – or for anything else. A heavy sleep after a heavy meal isn't good for you at all.

100

So what to do?

A simple exercise programme doesn't have to be fearsome at all. Begin by remembering that 'little and often' applies to exercise just as it does to eating. To solve the problem there is the *Gang of Four*.

The GANG OF FOUR are exercises that can be done by people of any age – yes, even by those who have stiff, arthritic joints, and even by those who find most exercises a dead bore and would hate to try anything strenuous.

Exercise – even gentle exercise – gives your metabolism a nudge in the right direction. These nudges add up, especially if you do them *after a meal*. This is where the gentleness is important.

Few people (except children) feel like being energetic after a meal. But when the therapy is gentle it only takes a little effort to accomplish metabolic wonders.

FINAL POINT. Our metabolism tends to slow down in the evening, balancing out with the morning 'wake up'. This is why nutritionists disapprove of our widespread habit to skimp breakfast, skimp lunch – and splurge in the evening. No doubt, another leave-over from our working lives; but now a habit that can be discarded.

Try to eat more at lunch, less at dinner. And even if you cannot achieve this all the time, try *very hard* to make the *Gang of Four* evening exercises as inevitable as possible.

You will be doing your metabolism a very big favour.

THE 'GANG OF FOUR' EXERCISES

Basically these are designed to stretch the muscles in your stomach, back, and neck. They will give a nice nudge to your metabolism. They will also improve your shape and help to make stiff joints more comfortable and flexible.

The first two can be done anywhere – when you're waiting for a bus, queuing at the supermarket, or just standing around in public or private.

NUMBER ONE – Stand with feet about six inches apart. Take a *deep* breath, pushing *out* your stomach – which is the opposite of what we normally do when we take a deep breath – and push the air you are taking in as far down in your stomach as possible.

Then draw the breath up through the diaphragm to the nostrils. Exhale slowly, bending the knees a little and pulling your stomach in and up hard. Imagine you are trying to tuck it under your chin.

Now straighten the knees and – without taking another breath – press the shoulders down, tense the muscles in your buttocks, and continue the upward pull on your stomach muscles. Stretch your neck, too, so that you are standing as tall as possible. Hold for a count of six.

Relax and take an easy breath. Repeat several times.

The same exercises can be done when you're sitting in a chair or lying in bed. You won't be able to bend the knees, but the breathing and stretching routine can be followed.

NUMBER TWO – Simply push out and pull in your stomach as *hard* and as *fast* as you can. Do this at least ten times. Allow a few moments of relaxation. Repeat two or three times.

This exercise can be done sitting or standing and is most desirable after a heavy meal.

NUMBER THREE – This divides into five quick and easy neck exercises. The stomach is also put to work.

a. Sit upright in a chair, facing forward. Breathe in deeply, as described in the first exercise, pushing *out* the stomach and then drawing the breath upwards. Stretch neck tall, and turn head as far as you can to the left, then to the right. Exhale as you turn and keep pulling the air up from your stomach. Then relax.

b. Breathe and stretch as in 'a'. Drop your head as far as you can, first to the left shoulder, then to the right. Do *not* raise your shoulder towards your head – the neck must do the work.

c. Breathe and stretch as before. Turn head to the left and drop chin on collarbone. Turn to the right and repeat.

d. Drop head backwards as far as it will go. Straighten slowly. Feel the upward pull on both neck and stomach muscles.

e. Drop head on chest. Rotate head slowly, first to the left, then to the right, stretching sideways and backwards as far as you can.

Older people often develop stiff necks. Don't push yourself too hard to begin with; just follow the routine whenever you have a spare moment and you should soon notice the loosening effect.

The routine also helps to relax tension, not only in the neck but through the whole body. Always do it when you have trouble sleeping.

NUMBER FOUR – Stand with feet apart. Clasp hands together and raise them straight above your head. Then S–t–r–e–t–c–h

Drop hands (still clasped) to the floor, bending at the waist. Now twist torso to the left as far as you can. Don't move feet, and you will feel pull on your waist muscles.

Raise hands slowly, performing an arc from the leftward bend to the starting position with arms straight above the head. And again S–t–r–e–t–c–h

Now repeat the bending as above, but to the right, and finish with the arms above the head.

Finally, unclasp your hands and bring arms down to your sides – stretching as you come, as if your hands were reaching out for some object just beyond their grasp.

If your waist needs a bit of trimming, this exercise will help.

★ ★ ★

A GRAND ANSWER

A young Frenchman once asked his grandmother when women stopped falling in love.
Her answer was that she had no idea.

★ ★ ★ ★

27
The Modern Disease

It begins with an 'A' – but you've probably guessed
wrong.

O NE of our friends, answering our questions on health,
observed:

'I have my problems. But, aged sixty-four, I don't think
AIDS is one of them.'

She's right. Anyone can run into Aids trouble with an emergency
blood transfusion in Africa. But, realistically, the chances are
remote. We do have health problems, but, at least, Aids is not
one of them.

ALLERGIES, a real modern disease, on the other hand, are
very much a problem, and they do not go away with age. Indeed,
they can get worse because we have lived with them for many
years without realizing what they are or how they are affecting
us.

There are obvious allergies, like hay fever, which are a clear
and immediate reaction to something hostile. In this case, pollen.
But there are many allergies which can be classified as 'hidden'.
The enemy does not trigger a quick reaction; it builds up a
malaise over months and years – often many years – and the
individual and, until recently, his or her doctor, does not know
why this malaise has been caused.

Doctors have long been baffled, and perhaps irritated, by
patients who say, 'I just don't feel WELL.' As age creeps on,
there's usually an explanation. Arthritis. Heart. Blood pressure.
Obesity. Even underweight. All too easy for a doctor to tell us, as

if we didn't know, that we are not as young as we were and can't expect always to feel like a spring chicken.

Now, modern medical science has discovered that a general don't-feel-well affliction need not have anything to do with age. It could have everything to do with an allergy, or allergies, we never knew about and, the good news is, which may be entirely curable.

Are allergies a common complaint?

You may be startled to learn that only ten percent of us are immune.

Some reactions are mild. So mild they can probably be ignored. But a lot of them are important and can make a very noticeable difference to our general health. This relatively new medical discovery makes it possible to identify – and therefore avoid – the 'hidden' enemies.

A few years ago these enemies could only be ascertained by the process of elimination. Try giving up eggs. Try giving up chocolate. Try giving up milk. And so on and so on. It took a long time and patients became extremely bored with it.

Now, however, doctors can arrange for a sophisticated blood test which pinpoints your particular troublemakers. They could be almost anything you eat or drink or, even, wear, and may come as a surprise to you. (Me allergic to chicken? Surely not?) But, at least, you know the answer quickly and can, equally fast, try the avoidance test. Medical experts assure us that improvement in health can be spectacular.

In most of the marriages we investigated there was one partner who grumbled more about his or her health than the other. Over the years the healthier partner had tended to become increasing deaf to complaints. In retirement, when such complaints can go Round the Clock, the choice is a) to become deafer still, or b) to fall back on the old chestnut, 'What can you expect at your age?'

But now the message to marriage partners is clear.

GET YOUR PARTNER TO TRY THE ALLERGY TEST. It's no big deal. And could help an amazing amount. There is no denying that better health Round the Clock contributes importantly to every aspect of your life together.

28
Enthusiasm

Can you still occasionally throw your hat in the air?

I N all of our interviews where we found what we considered a really successful marriage, we also found husbands and wives who still seemed to be able to generate a fair degree of enthusiasm.

For people who are not blessed with the inherent ability to be enthusiastic, you might possibly think that some kinds of enthusiasm we encountered were not merited – some even might be considered childish. And you may well be right.

As one wife told us, 'Last night Jack told me, "That's the best damned meat-loaf you have ever made." While even I thought it was a good meat-loaf, I know very well I have made better. But the fact Jack was so enthusiastic about it really delighted me.'

So if praise of a run-of-the-mill meat-loaf gives pleasure, enthusiasm about other little events can do likewise. Another example. We asked Humphrey L., who had mentioned that he enjoyed his wife's ability to be enthusiastic, to tell us the kind of things that her enthusiasm contributed to their marriage.

His reply was, 'Last Sunday, a miserable day, we went for a walk. On our return, Sue, as she was taking off her raincoat, said, "What wonderful fun it is to go for a walk in the rain."' And on another occasion we stopped in a bed-and-breakfast place that gave us the smallest room you can imagine. Not even room for a chair. I was a bit upset. But when Sue climbed into bed she almost shouted, "This is the most comfortable bed I've been in for years".'

Humphrey went on to say, 'She cheers me up. And I hope I do the same for her from time to time.'

It is much easier to show enthusiasm for a fancy birthday gift or a luxurious meal in a fine restaurant – although we heard private complaints that some wives and husbands don't even show much enthusiasm for such major events.

At the end of our research we discussed whether enthusiasm is something people are born with or can men and women who are not naturally enthusiastic develop the ability? And, in particular, can it be developed in later life?

We were forced to conclude that it is difficult for people who have gone through much of life without being naturally enthusiastic to get even marginally excited about anything as they grow older.

However, there were enough exceptions among the marriage partners with whom we talked to encourage us to report that it can be done. Both a Helen F. and a Mabel J. told us almost the same thing. 'After my husband retired I noted on those occasions when I was quite enthusiastic about something he did, how much it pleased him. So I started to make a conscious effort to be enthusiastic about something – no matter how small – more often. The silly thing is that very shortly I found that my enthusiastic outbursts not only made him feel better, but improved my own outlook. I can recommend it to any couple who are together a good deal.'

Others pointed out that in later years it is impossible to be enthusiastic when your arthritis is painful, or your budget is stretched to the breaking point, or when a friend dies. We agree.

But Helen and Mabel both said that if you can inject a little enthusiasm into your day-to-day living when life is going along relatively well it can be a most important ingredient in a successful marriage.

In our young days we often heard, 'An apple a day keeps the doctor away.' We would subscribe to the thought in retirement life that:

A BURST OF ENTHUSIASM A DAY, KEEPS THE
MARRIAGE COUNSELLORS AWAY

Also kept away, we are confident, would be divorce lawyers, psychiatrists, and, we would hazard a guess, the need for some doctors.

Enthusiasm is something we can recommend with a whole heart – without a single reservation.

Give it a try. You'll both enjoy it.

★ ★ ★ ★

A HANDY RECIPE

One certain way
To stop marriage tears –
Keep holding hands
For 40 years.

★ ★ ★ ★

29
Children

Can they be another case of role reversal?

WE liked the contribution from the son of one of our interviewees, Mark H., aged 45.

'A few months ago I took a bold decision. I told my father and mother that the time has come when parents should always obey their children. Not vice-versa. Of course it was partly a joke – but only partly.'

He approved our asking his parents about their reactions to this proposition.

His mother told us, 'I love my son dearly, but this joke – or half joke – made me very cross. The idea of parents being bossed around by their children reminded me of King Lear. It makes me feel gaga ahead of my time, and though I'm in my seventies, I'm not gaga at all.'

Later, the father responded quite differently, 'I was *delighted*. The idea of my son taking charge and organizing my life, the way I once organized his, was splendid. Perhaps I'm in my second childhood and need a stand-in father. But I wouldn't mind even if he told me what to eat for dinner. My wife does that anyway. So what's the difference?'

We quizzed other parents, and other sons and daughters, and found that these responses were quite usual. The older mothers disliked, sometimes detested, the idea of a vice-versa situation. Older fathers were far more relaxed and welcoming. We do not know how seriously they took the idea but, in theory at any rate, they had no violent objections.

So there seems to be quite a point of difference between couples with grown-up children.

There were, we concluded, two main reasons.

First, most mothers have been more actively involved in bringing up the family than the father. Mothers have loved them as babies, as toddlers, as tearabouts, even as adolescents; and the thought of them flying the nest has never been very acceptable. At any age they are still her little ones – and you don't take orders from 'little ones'.

The second reason we talked about in the topic 'WHO'S BOSS?'. Men, who have had to make decisions for most of their working lives, are often happy to hand over the responsibility when they retire. As Mark H's father indicates, husbands may see it as a choice between 'handing over' to their wife OR their children. And what's the difference?

Mothers, take note! The role of your children is an integral part of your marriage.

You may well find yourself taking on extra responsibility – not just for meals, but for many other decisions – in the years after your husband has retired. You may need help. More accurately, you probably will need help. And those 'little ones' who, like Mark H. could now be all of forty-five years old, are *the* people to give it.

Fathers, by and large, do not object to the offer of help from their offspring. We suggest that mothers learn to appreciate it too.

30
No-Go Areas

The mystery of the locked door.

ALEX and Maria had married in their twenties, produced three children, and, by and large, had made out pretty well together. When the children grew older, Maria trained, and then worked, as a social worker.

Alex worked for many years in the research department of a big commercial firm, and he was frankly secretive about many aspects of his job. Well, they *were* secret. Many competitive firms would have loved to know the secrets he knew.

So, there were several locked drawers in his desk at home and this did not worry Maria. She was busy with her own job and as she said, 'Even if I had read his secret documents, I wouldn't have understood them.'

Then they both retired and the drawers were unlocked. All except one.

Now that Maria had time on her hands, she began to get curious. She told us, 'There didn't seem a reason for the locked drawer. I knew he wasn't working on anything except his golf and I came right out and asked him why he still kept that drawer locked. He just shut me up. He said that it was none of my business.'

She admitted that it became something of an obsession. Was there a secret diary? Letters from a mistress – or even mistresses? Plans to leave home and start a new life? For heaven's sake, *what*?

Then she found the key. Alex was out and she went looking and it was surprisingly easy. The key was in the unlocked drawer where he kept his writing paper.

She opened the mysterious drawer and found – a notebook. It looked blank. She rifled through one empty page after another and then came on to a single entry in Alex's handwriting. 'NOTHING HERE. THIS WILL TEACH YOU TO GO SNOOPING.'

Maria re-locked the drawer, replaced the key with the writing paper. And then they never discussed it. As she told us, 'I had to laugh. It was so like Alex. He has this dry sense of humour and he's always been good at winning an argument by making it look *silly*.'

Was this his way of telling her that, even in retirement, you should keep at least one 'locked drawer'? Even if there is nothing important to hide?

The answer, of course, is yes.

But we must add a word of warning. Sometimes there *is* something important. Both husbands and wives have told us that they have found letters and other odd items – sometimes dated many years back – which still came as a shock. They *did* reveal relationships which may have been suspected but had never been spelled out in black and white.

Interestingly, both husbands and wives agreed that it would have been right to have maintained a private No-Go area.

Another story, however, was pretty scary. This concerned a couple who married after the husband had retired. She moved in to the home he had maintained for years. Soon, like Bluebeard's wife, the woman discovered a locked room – always locked – and she was told to keep out. In the end, of course, she found a way in and discovered rows and rows and rows of black leather garments. Many different shapes and sizes, but all glistening black.

She told us, 'I suppose I could just have ignored it. They weren't doing any harm. But the idea of living a retired life with a man who had a secret fetish just destroyed me. It was so creepy – so unlike my first husband who had been as normal as sunshine.'

She took her problem to a psychologist and he did little to reassure her. He even warned that it is impossible to tell where these fetishes might lead. 'If you tried to talk this out with your new husband it could be he would try to strangle you with one of his black leather belts.'

She decided on divorce. Here was a No-Go area that she just couldn't live with.

In general, though, our research showed up nothing worse than a reasonable desire for *some* privacy – and this desire certainly showed up stronger after retirement. This makes sense. Both husbands and wives can feel that all areas are being 'invaded' now that the two of them are together so much of the time – and they do not necessarily like it.

There seems to be a difference in attitude here between the sexes. For the wives, No-Go areas are largely physical – doors, drawers, rooms, etc.. However, for the husbands, No-Go areas have more to do with talk – subjects that they do not want to talk about.

When the Duke of Windsor went into early retirement, the Duchess loyally maintained, in public, that all-day togetherness made for the best marriage. She certainly had it. The Duke followed her like a shadow and, in private, she admitted that it could be trying. She was a woman who spent a lot of time on her make-up, her nails, her hair, her clothes. And quite simply, she did not want the Duke lurking in her dressing room when all of this was going on. She would send him on errands and once even confided to a friend that nobody knew how much trouble she took, in her words, '. . . to keep the little man busy.'

Most wives would see her point. (Even if they felt she was being ungrateful to a man who had given up a throne for her sake.) They do not want a husband hanging about when they are trying out a new girdle, a new hair tint, or dyeing their eyelashes. A degree of physical privacy matters.

One husband, however, was speaking for many when he told us, 'There are certain things I just don't want to discuss. My wife wonders why I didn't get along with my father. She would like to rake over the reasons for the break-up of my first marriage. She would like to know if I had homosexual relationships at school. And I just feel it's private. There are plenty of other subjects I am happy to discuss with her. But not everything.'

So it looks as if retired couples must have a particular respect for No-Go areas. With so much extra time available, they may be tempted to spend some of this extra time trying to invade what had been for years their partners' accepted No-Go areas.

But our advice is – *resist* it.

A good marriage does not mean you have to get into every corner and crevice of each other's lives.

Sometimes, indeed, a good retirement marriage may depend on keeping out.

31
Quarrels

. . . and do men sulk more than women?

WE have had so many discussions – although not quite quarrels – on this subject, we have decided to write our separate viewpoints.

First, here's Phoebe's

Quarrels are an aspect of retirement which seems to have taken quite a few of our friends and respondents by surprise.

Like post-natal depression or arguments about changing nappies, most couples felt that quarrels were a problem which belonged to the earlier days of marriage. Just conceivably, there were husbands and wives who 'never had a cross word' even in their tempestuous youth. But in general, quarrels, even full-blooded ones, were felt to be part of life. As one husband said, 'I don't think you can get to know each other properly without them.'

But they tend to simmer down as the years go on and as the children – a fruitful source of dissention – grow up and move out. Partners learn to adapt, to make concessions. They probably learn to avoid controversial matters because they realize that you can't always solve them.

Perhaps, too, we have a feeling that it is a bit – well, undignified for granny and grandpa to quarrel. We ought to be past such things.

Then along comes retirement, and granny and grandpa are disconcerted to find they're not past it at all. On the contrary:

disagreements that had simmered down begin to boil up. They may well be quarrelling more often, more violently than they have done for years.

Marion T. wrote:

> Sometimes I almost had to laugh. They were so like the arguments we had when we were first married. Usually starting with something quite small and silly.
>
> Here's an example. Charles was a tidy young man and he hated coming home to an untidy house. I didn't blame him for that; but sometimes he would nit-pick about stupid things, like the wastepaper basket being in the wrong place, and I'd get mad and there would be a full-scale quarrel.
>
> Then it eased off. Maybe he became more tolerant or I became more careful, or we just grew more used to each other. And when the kids came along he accepted that an immaculate home was not always possible. But there came this day, soon after he retired, when he had been off watching a football game, and he came home to find the living room a bit of a mess. (I had been out most of the day too.) So he said something like, 'For God's sake, what do you have to do all day but keep the place tidy?' And I blew my top and shouted back, 'For God's sake, what do *you* have to do but watch football?' And what a humdinger we had then!
>
> Afterwards, we were quite shocked. We both felt we were too old for that kind of thing. But we weren't.

It may help Marion to realize how many other retired couples have the same problem. (A lot of people do not appreciate this because older couples become better at concealing their quarrels from every one except themselves. So never be deceived by an appearance of harmony. It could conceal exactly the same blast-offs as your own.)

That's the first thing. And it is not difficult to see why the trouble should happen. Without making too many excuses for crabbiness or quick tempers, it is fair to remember that, in some ways, when retirement comes along we have to get used to each other all over again. It is not all that different from those first married years.

On both occasions couples have to get into a new routine. A notoriously difficult thing to do. All right, they are not going to feel strangers the way just-marrieds can do. On the other hand, they are less adaptable than the young, perhaps not enjoying vibrant health, and less inclined to make allowances, and – worst of all – less inclined to kiss and make up.

This may be a purely feminine view but we have found that a lot of wives feel that men are the sulkier sex. A woman will often confess to being the one who goes in for confrontation, who starts the shouting. And they are not proud of it. The undignified 'not-for-granny' aspect worries them. But they point out that you cannot shout for long, whereas sulking can go on indefinitely.

We found support in our research for the argument that the sulky husband may well get sulkier when he retires. The younger man, hurrying off to work, has plenty to distract him. There is a fair chance that he will have forgotten, or nearly forgotten, what the quarrel was about when he gets home. But when he sits home all day there is a chance he may brood and sulk even longer.

What to do?

The wife can console herself, remembering that many other retired wives are looking at the equally gloomy I'm-not-talking-to-you kind of face. She knows he will come out of it in time. But most women like to break through and get things back to normal as soon as possible.

One wife we know did something that was absurdly, brilliantly right. Her mate, now retired, had hardly spoken to her, after a quarrel, for several days. The conventional, 'I'm sorry dear' – 'I know a lot of it was my fault' – 'Can't we forget it?' had not worked at all.

So the next morning she came down to breakfast in an extraordinary old dress that had belonged to her grandmother. It was all gold – from top to bottom. She had added every piece of gold costume jewelry she owned – and had found some kind of gold turban for her head. Before he could stop himself the husband said, 'What in the world are you up to?' She quietly answered, 'If silence is golden, that is the way I am going to look. I'll wear this outfit all morning until the plumber comes; and I'll wear it this evening when we go out to dinner. If any one asks me why, I'll tell him.'

You've guessed it. He smiled. And every time he managed to stop, he saw her frying eggs at the stove in her all-gold outfit, and he smiled again.

So that became their code. Whenever he looked like getting into a sulk, she would say, 'Want me to get out that gold dress?' They both admit it still works.

But in case we cannot all come up with such weird and successful ideas, let's ask Joe for some practical, man's view advice. Most of us agree that sulking is the worst part of quarrelling, so how can we cope with it? Men as well as women?

Now, here's Joe:

OK, Phoebe. As we said at the beginning we do not want to have a quarrel on this subject. But I have talked with a cross section of men – mostly about my age – and I found absolutely no support for your argument that men sulk more than women.

I did sense some agreement that men tend to 'go into their shell' rather more than women after a marital misunderstanding – and stay there longer.

I can hear you right now asking, 'What's the difference between sulking – and going into a shell?'

A good question. I tried to pry a convincing answer out of my male respondents – and had very little success. Most men do claim that being accused of 'sulking' was an irritating insult that upset them – while they considered 'going into a shell' for a period was not all that bad in that it was a position they took to prevent what could be a minor quarrel from becoming a flaming fight.

They, by and large, agreed that men, compared to women, prefer to avoid out-and-out confrontations and that 'going into a shell' could stop a small bush blaze from becoming a fully-fledged forest fire. (Incidentally – but, perhaps, not so incidentally – there was almost unanimous agreement with your thought that women are more prone to initiate disagreements – and they also agreed that women worked harder at terminating them.)

However, all of my male respondents also agreed, as you point out, the loss of a day-by-day job to go to, where the reason for going into their shell used to be crowded out of their minds, made for retirement marriage quarrels lasting longer.

I guess that I should also tell you an amusing side of my particular research project. In group interviews, where five or six of us were sitting around a table, we had much fun trying to figure out the relationship between the time men stayed in their shell after some family problem – and the importance of the subject of the quarrel.

Phoebe, as a woman, you probably know the answer, but we had to admit to each other that the more serious the disagreement, the less time men spent in their shell. And vice-versa – the more petty the subject, the longer we seem to stay there. Of course, this isn't sulking, is it Phoebe?

The moral for wives must be, therefore, only have quarrels about important matters. You husband will be back to normal much sooner.

Finally, and regretfully, all the husbands agreed, as I am sure wives would, that in the early days of marriage the finest solution to marital quarrels was some quiet love making. As a solution to the problem of getting a man out of his shell – or even sulking – there was, and is, no better way.

In those days two or three – or more – family arguments could be solved every week. Later on this solution is no longer available with anywhere near the same frequency.

OUR JOINT CONCLUSION

We would like to impress on wives the value of being sensitive, even super-sensitive, to those small items that upset their husbands. Minor disagreements can look like a major issue.

And we would like to impress on husbands that sometimes they *do* spend more time 'in their shells' than is strictly necessary. If the wife is trying to coax him out with a view toward reconciliation, it just might be called sulking if he refuses to emerge. The reasonable need for protection, for avoiding a worse disagreement, is over and neither partner should be in the punishment business – the 'you did this to *me* so I'm going to get back at *you*' attitude. When you are retired, life is, quite literally, too short.

It would help, too, if men recognized that an occasional flare-up can be something of a physical necessity for women. It is not a virtue, any more than sneezing your head off is a virtue. But it happens; and it need not do harm *if* the husband is prepared to forgive and forget sooner rather than later.

So let us recognize that it is impossible to have a retirement marriage without some disagreements, some irritation, some upsets. But if they can come and go without either party becoming bitter, marriages can continue to be most satisfactory the whole way.

Both of us would like to stress one point again because we see it as crucial. All of us should keep on remembering that we only have a limited time left to resolve arguments. The sooner we solve them, the more time we have left to enjoy life together.

★ ★ ★

NO ARGUMENT HERE

There was an old lady of Fife
With a fondness for marital strife
    She said 'At my age
    To have a good rage
Is a way to add spice to my life.'

★ ★ ★

ROYAL ADVICE

'The nice thing about grandchildren is that you can spoil them with a clear conscience.'

The Queen Mother

32
Quirks

and do we get quirkier as we get older?

B AD news.
    Everybody has some quirks. Yes, you have some – and so does your mate.

But first, just what is a quirk? The dictionary says it is 'a peculiarity in action, behaviour, or personality; mannerism'. And it is interesting that both husbands and wives tell us that their mates have some quirks, while they themselves might have one or two – but no more.

Further, it would seem that one's own quirks are harmless, while your spouse's are, more often than not, annoying.

One husband, a retired schoolteacher, has a quirk about bank statements – in particular, his wife's. Each month he goes into paroxysms of anger when his wife mumbles, 'Oh well. My account is only three pounds and fifty pence out – and the bank is always right – so I won't bother.'

A red flag to a bull does less to the bull's aggression than this monthly announcement does to this normally even-tempered husband. He then spends an hour figuring out where the missing money went – and always finds that the bank *is* right. But if his wife repeats her comment the next month, he goes through the whole routine again. He has a quirk – and furthermore, he knows it.

Or a wife we know has a quirk about a milk bottle or carton on the dining table. To avoid this cataclysm she will put some milk in a jug, put the jug on the table, put a few drops into her husband's coffee (she doesn't take milk), pour the remainder of the milk back into the bottle, and then her husband has to wash the jug. She admits that she has a definite peculiarity on this subject.

The husband claims he recognizes his wife's quirk on the subject of milk containers on the table, but even after 43 years he forgets and occasionally puts a bottle on the table – with upsetting consequences.

Unfortunately, it is much easier to spot your partner's quirks than it is to spot your own. On the other hand it is just as important to recognize the quirks that your partner has and then do your best not to infringe or become unduly upset by them. This is even more important – and fortunately is somewhat easier to do.

If your husband gets upset with your monthly announcement about your inaccurate bank balance, it is probably better not to make any audible announcement about the inbalance. (He will no doubt find out in time – but three or four outbursts a year are a lot better than twelve.)

And as for milk on the dining table, the husband should recognize that this does produce 'a peculiarity in behaviour' and either give up putting milk in his coffee or resign himself to washing 365 dirty jugs during the year.

A wide range of quirks were revealed in our discussions with retired couples. For example, one wife cannot abide a picture on a wall to be even minimally askew. She will go into a neighbour's

home, walk over to a picture that is fractionally uneven, and straighten it. She admits that what often appears to be uneven to her, looks absolutely even to everyone else.

In her own home the pictures are balanced daily. But this no longer bothers her husband of 38 years as he has become used to straight pictures – and tells us that he, too, has begun to straighten them – and at friends' homes. So quirkiness can be catching.

On the other hand one husband, reporting on his own quirks, told us that nothing infuriates him more than having his wife perpetually brush imaginary, he thinks, specks from his shoulders every time he puts on a dark sweater or jacket. He recognizes that this is a quirk of hers and he tries, successfully for the most part, to hold his tongue while his wife flicks at his shoulders with the back of her hand.

One fairly common quirk has to do with, of all things, the arrival time at airports and train stations – even bus terminals – when travelling.

We were amazed to learn how many wives reported that their husbands have a quirk about the absolute necessity of getting to the departure point up to three hours ahead of the scheduled time – while other wives report that their husbands think it absolutely necessary to arrive, panting, no more than a few seconds before the gates close.

Both groups readily admitted that their concept of the acceptable time to arrive was a true peculiarity in personality. They all felt strongly about their own concept, and they were equally open that their concept probably had no basis in reality.

However, we should report one wife's tale – which she swears is true. Her husband insisted on arriving at the airport so far in advance of the scheduled departure time for a long-planned holiday trip that, after checking in, they went to a nearby cinema and saw most of a movie – a re-run of *Gone with the Wind* – and still confortably made their flight. Honestly, that's her story.

Another wife told us of one of her own quirks. She sees red when her husband puts salt on his food before tasting it. She agrees that if he wants some salt, it is up to him, and she should not get upset. But she does.

It was not so bad for the first 40 years of their marriage when he was working as a telephone lineman and often had to work odd hours. She watched him put salt on his meal perhaps only four or five times a week.

Now she sees him do it almost twenty-one times a week, and she has trouble containing her feelings. She confessed that recently she put half a teaspoon of salt into one serving of peas before she put them on his plate. Of course, without tasting them, he added his usual amount of salt.

What was his reaction?

He did not notice. (We should add that he is 75 and in excellent health. She is 65 and has high blood pressure. She thinks her high blood pressure results from *her* quirk concerning *his* salt.)

When we were doing our interviews we asked the question whether people thought they became more susceptible to quirks as they grow older – and the answer was almost always an emphatic yes. That's the bad news.

The good news is that it was felt in long-term marriages each partner became more tolerant of the other's quirks as the years roll by. So the net result evens out; more quirks but, at the same time, more tolerance, so the total problem does not seem to change.

Finally, three quite serious observations about quirks.

First, all quirks are disturbing in some degree to the other partner – especially in retirement marriages. Further, they can be equally disturbing to the one that has the quirk and recognizes and acknowledges it.

Second, as mentioned above most husbands and wives admitted that they might have a few minor 'mannerisms', but the spouse had 'quirks'. We concluded that, regardless of what they are called, both partners usually possess equivalent amounts. So we suggest that you be aware of your partner's quirks; and just try to live with them.

Third, do not let the presence of quirks upset your marriage. Every marriage has them.

33
Pets

You may have something in common with the Royal Family.

A recent author, writing on retirement, had a chapter on pets which was titled 'PET HATES'. He, as you might guess, was against them – basically because they were a tie and prevented their owners from enjoying the freedom of action which, by rights, should be theirs.

He does, of course, have a point. The freedom to leave home for a day, a week, a month is curtailed when there are dogs or cats or birds to be considered. Maybe you have obliging neighbours who will cope with the food and the exercising.

Or, perhaps, you have friends who will actually take your pets into their own homes while you are away. But not everyone is that lucky; and if you are fond of your animals, arrangements for their well-being every time you leave home can be a headache.

And yet . . . and yet . . . Well, maybe you are one of those couples who do have something in common with the Royal Family.

Everyone knows the Queen adores her corgis. Her first beloved pet, Susan, went with her on her honeymoon. (As it was a cold November day a hot water bottle was put in the carriage to keep Susan warm.) On the day of Queen Victoria's Coronation she found time to give her spaniel, Dashy, a bath.

Charles II loved birds; and when a favourite crane broke its leg, he arranged for it to be fitted with an artificial limb. The Duke of Windsor always allowed his cairn terrier, Cora, to sleep on his bed. And when Cora became too stiff to jump up, special steps were installed so that she could walk up to bed.

Queen Alwxandra, wife of Edward VII, went to a sale and returned with several cats, a puppy, a flying fox, two kids, and a marmoset. (They all spent their first night in a spare bedroom at Buckingham Palace.)

These stories could go on forever. And we are not just illustrating a fact that some people love animals. (Obvious.) There are special reasons why the Royal Family should love them – and the reasons are not so different when you look at the relationship between pets and retired couples.

Can you guess?

Queen Elizabeth II put her finger on it when she said, 'Animals don't know you're anything different. They just love you for yourself.' It is easy to see how Royals – who have to be treated as 'somebody special' by everyone around them – should find the uncomplicated affection of a corgi very refreshing.

In the same way, animals do not know you are growing older. They don't count the wrinkles or grey hairs. They don't notice if you start wearing spectacles or stop wearing youthful slimline clothes. If you cannot dance the night away or collect a Latin lover – what do they care? As the Queen says; they just love you for yourself; and they will never notice that it's an older self.

All our reports suggest that there *is* a special relationship between older people and animals. But, like most generaliza-

tions, there are exceptions to the rule – for example, many older people don't like animals at all. So we feel that pets are an area where couples should make allowances for each other.

We certainly heard a few horror stories; like the wife who reported that, after retirement, her husband became more and more besotted with dogs. At the time of our interview they had six – including a Great Dane – who all slept on their bed.

Another true bedroom story: one husband complained that his wife liked to sleep with four hens and a bantam cock.

Obviously, 'special relationships' with pets can go too far.

More commonly we found in some families there was an imbalance in the attitude to pets. One partner liked them better than the other and there was considerable aggro when the animal lover allowed a cat to claw the upholstery, or a muddy dog to walk across a new carpet.

It would help to some degree if the non-animal-lover appreciated the reasons why the spouse should be so attached to a pet. It is human and understandable, just as Charles II's affection for his crippled crane was human and understandable.

Further, we should accept that the older we get the stronger the attachment may become. (At her death Queen Victoria had 82 dogs.)

But as we said in our topic on ECCENTRICS do not push your love of pets too far. Six dogs, including a Great Dane, on the bed is altogether unreasonable.

34
Sleeping

. . . and does the time come for separate rooms?

ONE couple we interviewed reported that they celebrated their Golden Wedding Anniversary by buying a new double bed. The husband observed that we know the slogan, 'Families who pray together, stay together.' But he would like to add, 'Couples who sleep together, keep together.'

He has a point. Sex comes into it, of course: sex and physical affection. (Other topics in this book discuss the importance of both.) At any time in a marriage, the shared bedroom is, at least, some proof of marital stability.

It is said that Gerald and Betty Ford were the first U.S. President and his wife who shared a double bed at the White House. This confirmed the feeling among the American public that they were a very devoted couple. It met with general approval.

One must accept. however, that older couples *can* have problems if they share the same room, let alone the same bed. Very often we found that the reason had nothing to do with loss of affection, physical or otherwise. More likely it is because our sleeping patterns tend to change with age.

We sleep easily for short periods. When there is no work calling us back in the afternoon, the post-lunch nap becomes routine. But a long, uninterrupted sleep through the night is more of a rarity.

This is disturbing, particularly when you have been a good sleeper most of your life. Doctors are besieged with complaints about insomnia and may hand out sleeping pills, but they often add that they are not a perfect solution. If nature has decided that a night-long sleep is not for you, it is better to accept the fact and try to adapt.

How?

Well, the worst thing you can do is lie, tense and aggrieved, in the darkness thinking, 'I ought to be asleep.' Far better to read a book, listen to music or news on the radio, perhaps get up and make yourself a cup of soothing tea. A break like this will often send you back to sleep and you'll wake up feeling fine.

The trouble of course is – *your partner*. Maybe he or she also wakes up, but not necessarily at the same time. Anyone who is asleep won't welcome a disturbance. Lights turned on, pages rustled, radio filling the bedroom air – all unacceptable.

Then there's snoring. (This can happen any time. The press reported recently that a 19-year-old bride spent most of her honeymoon nights in the bathtub with a blanket.) But the decibels do seem to rise with the years and one partner may feel, understandably, that the time has come to move out. 'It's not that I don't love you, dear, but . . . .'

We found quite a few couples who had made this decision and there certainly is no reason to feel embarrassed or guilty. Others felt that, sooner or later, the step will become inevitable. But if you are wondering whether or not it is a good idea, we would like you to consider the case of a couple in their mid-seventies.

Dave and Miriam N. decided on separate bedrooms. They had moved into a small house where there were three bedrooms – but one hardly more than a cupboard. They liked to have their children and grandchildren come to stay. Miriam admitted, 'It wasn't a very romantic reason for us to get back in the same bed together, but it kept happening – simply because there wouldn't have been room for the family.'

Then something else happened. The came to realize that they missed the closeness, the companionship through the night. When the family's visit ended they both decided to leave the second bedroom unoccupied.

The problems did not change. They both snored at times; they both had nocturnal habits which might wake the other. But as Dave told us, 'We learned to accommodate. We agreed never to turn on the light. Never to make any noise. If I wanted to read I would creep down to the living room. Miriam bought a pair of earphones which she could slip on in the dark and listen to the radio – or her special Relaxation Tape.

'Sometimes I would steal out, quiet as a thief, and find Miriam already in the kitchen making tea. We would have a cup together and return to bed. It was almost fun.'

As for their snoring, Miriam said, 'You can give a nudge, ask the other to turn over. Or I can just consider it traffic noise and get used to it.'

We suggest that it might be a good idea for couples, who have retreated to separate bedrooms, to try the occasional get-together. Like Dave and Miriam, they should agree on specific bedroom rules – ones that would not have been necessary when they were young, sound sleepers.

It can be nice to feel your partner is there, right beside you. Like Dave and Miriam you might decide to make it permanent – again.

A PS FROM JOE

Audrey and I are still in the single bedroom, double bed group. But I must admit we now have a king sized bed. It is only a foot or two larger than a regular double bed – but, oh, that little extra space gives me room to revolve, rotate, and generally gyrate during the night without disturbing Audrey too much. I hope.

I'd almost sell the dog before selling our king sized bed.

35
Correcting

'No, it was in 1963, not 1964.'

WE certainly reaped a whirlwind in over half of our interviews when we asked, 'Does your husband – or wife – ever
correct you when you are relating some incident – either when
you are with friends or when you are alone?'

We were amazed at the number of affirmative answers and
particularly the strength of emotion that the subject aroused.
The complainants were almost equally split between husbands
and wives – and in quite a few households both partners felt that
they each were corrected in mid-sentence far too often.

A Mrs. F – we won't identify her further lest her husband
correct what she told us – said, 'We have been married 42 years
and since we are now together much more, his habit of interrup-
ting me to amend some very minor detail about what I am saying
really upsets me. For example, I can hear him now saying, "Dear,
we have only been married just over 41 and a half years." He's
usually right; and I know that sometimes I am not all that
accurate, but what bugs me is that his corrections are usually very
unimportant.'

A husband voiced almost exactly the same observation. 'Ann
seems to take delight in making sure what I am saying is
absolutely precise – when it really doesn't make much difference.
Yesterday I was talking on the telephone with a friend and I said
something about our getting a dog last July, and I heard Ann,
who was in the room at the time, mumble audibly that it was not
July, but in June. She's probably right, but it's an unimportant
detail so far as my friend is concerned – or for the dog either,

who is still not house-trained and we have had him a month longer than I had thought.'

We sat down and tried to think why this habit of correcting unimportant details seems to be so much more prevalent in long-term marriages. The answer we came up with is twofold. First, husbands and wives are talking in each other's presence much more often than previously. And therefore there are that many more details being spoken which could be slightly inaccurate.

Second, when you have been married 42 years – even 41 and a half – you have a greater amount of common knowledge information on which one partner, or the other, can err a bit. When you have been married just five years, most of what is being discussed concerns a time before you knew each other – and as a consequence those details being reported as facts have to be accepted as 100% accurate.

None of our respondents claimed to be annoyed when they are corrected for saying something far off the mark. It was the same Mrs. F. we quoted above who told us frankly, 'Last month Bill heard me telling the man at the garage we were having trouble with the alternator, and could he put it right. Bill corrected me quickly, pointing out it was the carburettor, not an alternator, that was the problem. Obviously, I appreciate an important correction like this one.'

The real problem in this area lies completely with small details, often very small details. If a man says he weighs 12 stone, there is little to be gained by pointing out he really weighs 12 stone two. Or, if a wife claims she can knit a sweater in a month, the husband should restrain himself and not point out the one he has on took six weeks.

If you do not have a 'correcting' problem in your home you might think these examples are ridiculous. Sorry, but they are true.

In those homes where there is one, or two, impulsive correctors, we strongly recommend that some self-control be exercised. The habit is more annoying than you might think. If the correction is basically unimportant, we suggest you let it quietly pass.

Correcting

Finally, we found that the correcting habit is a very noticeable-to-others mannerism. We were told on more than one occasion, 'We have a friend, Jack J. who is constantly correcting his wife. We would think it must be obvious to him what he is doing. But he keeps on, to the point where we are embarrassed.'

The 'correcting' habit may not be quite as obvious as the habit some couples have of constantly bickering in public. But if you do have the correcting habit, your partner is certainly aware of it – and so are all of your close friends. So it is probably worthwhile trying to correct the habit, rather than your spouse.

36
Divorce

After forty years?

IT is reported that a certain Indian lady, suspecting her husband of infidelity, murdered him in a particularly gruesome way. First, she administered a powerful sleeping drug. Then she trussed him like a chicken. Finally, she cut him up into a hundred pieces.

During her trial she maintained there was nothing else a lady in her position could have done. Counsel for the Prosecution pointed out that there was such a thing as divorce. The lady sighed deeply, and replied, 'Ah yes. But divorce is so *painful*.'

She had a point. Divorces may now be as common as tax demands, but the number that can be described as 'painless' remains obstinately low. Nor is there any evidence that it gets less painful as we get older. Different – yes. From our evidence we believe that positions are now often reversed. In earlier years it is the wife who finds divorce harder to take; later on, it could well be the husband.

There are a number of reasons for this. By nature, women are the more sentimental or emotional; more likely to be devastated when love's young dream goes down the drain. As a rule she is left to cope with the children – a time-consuming business and not easy to combine with a normal working or social life. Loneliness can be a big problem.

The man is relatively unfettered (except by alimony). He can re-marry or resume a bachelor life. Work goes on much as before. And although there are adjustments to be made, the total sense of change and upheaval which afflicts the wife is far less likely to come his way.

But leap ahead into Senior Citizen years and the picture changes. Yes, we know that Man can still remain the Wanderer; there have been septuagenarians who have taken to the hills with a blonde barmaid; leaving behind faithful grey-haired wives to whom they have been married for forty years. But let's be realistic. Ninety-nine per cent of older husbands are going to do no such thing.

On the contrary: man becomes more and more dependent on a stable and familiar home with a stable and familiar wife, faults and all. This may not stop him criticising and complaining, but try taking her away. Soon he is desperate to have her, faults and all, back.

And the wife?

She, too, comes to depend on the stability and the familiarity. But it is well known that widows cope with their lives better than widowers. As the wife of a famous Oxford professor once said, 'If I were to get hit by a bus, Harold would have to re-marry within a week.' (And their children were in unqualified agreement.)

Their marriage was a happy one and no wife could have been more devoted. But later, she herself survived twelve years of widowhood very successfully. Nobody was surprised.

By now you will have seen that this book recognizes that there are many real marriage problems after retirement. Many of them can be serious – and most of our correspondents agree.

A Maria F. wrote, 'If anyone had told me that I would be thinking about divorce for the first time after thirty-nine years, I would think they had to be joking. But it's happened and I can't even give you very good reasons. We just seem to grate on each other's nerves, and I can't stomach so much grating so many hours of the day.'

While Chris M. admitted, 'In our first two years of retirement, I think I talked about divorce four times.'

In some ways, divorce in later years seems an easier proposition. There are no young children to worry about; and as one couple observed, 'We had decided to move house and settle in another part of the country, so re-settling in two houses didn't look like a big problem. We were told, too, that older couples

were likely to be calmer, more reasonable, about the separation.'
DON'T YOU BELIEVE IT!

Such comments came from couples thinking about divorce. Those who had actually done the deed sounded very different. It was far more painful that they had expected. Sorting out two lives which had been entangled so long, had not proved easy — still less unemotional. Although the children had grown up, they had still been shocked and upset. And the word 'lonely' came up again and again.

As we said earlier, we believe that men were the worse affected. They just could not cope with running a home on their own; and if they settled in a new area they found it much harder than women to make new friends. If they re-married, it was often in a spirit of some desperation, and it did not always prove happy.

In our opinion, no one can lay down hard and fast rules about divorce at any time of life. Sometimes it may be the best thing to do. *but men beware*. It is more likely to work out for you early in life; and in retirement, you might do better to adopt the attitude of a friend of ours who told us that he thought about murder often, divorce never.

Like the Indian lady, he has a point.

FEELING SHEEPISH?

Mary had a little man,
  His hair was white as snow,
And everywhere that Mary went
  Her mate was sure to go.

She loved him very tenderly
  For hours in every day
But there were hours when she did wish
  That he would GO AWAY.

Anon

37
Grandchildren

Blessings – or otherwise?

MANY, if not most, retirement marriages are blessed with grandchildren – from one to twenty-three. (At least that is the largest number any of our interviewees claimed.)

On the surface everyone says they are pleased with their grandchildren. But under the surface we found that in many cases grandchildren generate some friction in their grandparents' marriage.

How?

We found that all grandchildren can be divided into two distinct groups. Not, in this case, male and female. But rather those ten years old and younger, and those eleven or older. Give or take a year or so on either side.

The younger group of grandchildren are a great boon to almost every marriage. By and large the under ten group love their grandparents, are nice to their grandparents, and most importantly they give their grandparents an outside interest. Almost always the major interest that a couple has in common.

However, when grandchildren approach their teens – and for four or five years thereafter – their positive effect on their grandparents more often than not takes on a new light. As one grandmother admitted to us – and she was so sensitive on the point she asked us not to identify her in any way – 'Until Billy was thirteen he was the apple of our eye. But one day he came to visit us and his hair was down the back of his neck – and horror or horrors he was wearing an earring. My husband lost his temper, and the next thing I knew we were having a terrible row – all because of Billy's earring.'

She caught her breath for a moment and then continued, 'My husband was all for calling our daughter and laying down the law by insisting Billy could never come to our house again with that damned earring. I tried, I think tactfully, to convince him that if he did he would then have a row with both his wife *and* his daughter – and probably his son-in-law. And, in the end, not change anything in regard to the earring. A big price to pay for no result.'

This story was repeated often but with various other complaints. You would not think that eye shadow on a thirteen-year-old granddaughter could upset a grandparents' marriage. Or that the inadvertent use of a four letter word by a fourteen-year-old – which he claimed, rightfully, he had heard often on TV – so incensed one grandmother she had to take to her bed; leaving her 82-year-old husband to prepare dinner for himself – and his erring grandson. Even she admitted that it was not the stuff of which successful marriages are made.

Our conclusion is no different than that reached by all of the couples whose marriage has been upset from time to time by grandchildren. They all agreed that it was foolish to lose much sleep because of something over which they had no control – and, in truth, no direct responsibility. We recognize that this is easy to say, but is more difficult to accomplish.

There was no doubt that they all had a real interest in their grandchildren but if the latter had habits which either the grandmother or the grandfather – or both – did not approve, it was OK to state their disapproval but from then on the subject should be dropped.

For those of you who have grandchildren we suggest the following rule:

LOVE, LOVE, LOVE YOUR GRANDCHILDREN UNTIL THEY ARE ABOUT TEN – DEVELOP SOMETHING OF A BLIND EYE UNTIL THEY ARE SEVENTEEN – BE PROUD OF THEM EVERMORE.

A PS FROM PHOEBE

I think there is an important role which grandparents can, very successfully, play.

In many families there is a child who is not quite the favourite. He or she may be more difficult, less attractive, less bright than the others; and even though the parents may try very hard to make no distinctions and have no favourites . . . . well, it isn't always easy.

Grandparents can often spot the problem and adjust the balance. They are detached enough to make a conscious decision that their favourite – ie the one that get that little extra attention, treats, displays of affection – is the one who does not get it from the parents.

Some old friends of mine achieved this special relationship with a grandson who a) had a pronounced squint, b) failed most of his exams, and c) went through a phase where he wore not only an earring but also a long pigtail.

Now that the grandson is in his early 20's, he says that this supportive relationship with his grandparents made a major difference in his life.

38
Memory

If you're worried about your memory, forget it!

Good news! Forgetfulness does not cause much strife between retired husbands and wives.

So how can an understanding of a seeming loss of memory help a marriage?

Before answering that question we should report that we studied the problem after the subject came up in almost every interview with both partners who were over 60.

As Helen N. put it, 'I am often depressed because I seem to be unable to remember things as well as I used to. And when I'm depressed I am not much of a wife to Henry – and he tells me that he has the same problem.'

Or as dozens of husbands said in essence, 'I'm so embarrassed because I have to keep asking my wife such questions as "What's the name of my cousin who lives in Leeds?" or, "Who were those nice people we enjoyed so much when we were on holiday?" or "What day next week are we supposed to baby-sit for the grandchildren?"'

We have more news for you. Almost everyone over 60 has this problem – and almost everyone worries about it. Many of the men and women who mentioned their increasing forgetfulness would ask us, 'Am I getting senile?' and even more often, 'Do you think I'm getting Alzheimer's disease?'

And we have more news for them – and for you, if you are one of those who worry about becoming more forgetful. You are *not* getting senile – and the medical profession tells us that the incidence of Alzheimer's disease is so small that any one who is aware enough to ask whether they have the disease is certainly not suffering from it.

All of us see our hair turn grey. We may not like it all that much, but we do not worry about it because this is what has happened to hair for the last four thousand years. The same is true with what we all think is a loss of memory when we get older. This too has been going on for many centuries and should cause about as much concern as greying hair.

There is a precise reason for what you think is your loss of memory problem.

And this is the reason. When you were twenty-years-old your brain had been exposed to a certain number of, let's call them, 'units of information'. A unit is somebody's name, the author of a book you had read, movies you had seen, a fact you had learned in biology class at school, a joke, an historical fact, a telephone number, or whatever.

By your twentieth birthday you had been exposed, let's say, to a million different units of information – and without doubt you had forgotten 90% of them. Nine hundred thousand things had been forgotten. But you weren't worried. You probably were not even aware that you had forgotten them.

For example, even at the age of twenty, do you think you could have remembered the names of all the students in your first class at school? Or the details of all the books you had read in school? Or the names of all the shops your mother took you to when you were a child?

Of course not. No one, not even a genius, could remember all the units of information we absorb in our daily lives. It would take a vast modern computer to store all the data that you and I, average citizens, have known at one time. And we are not computers.

From age twenty to forty you were exposed not to just one additional million units of information but probably three million more. So at age forty you had forgotten 90% of four million units. That's three million, six hundred thousand things you had forgotten. And you still were not worried.

And from forty to sixty you added another three million – that makes seven million – and your forgetfulness rate stays the same

– 90%. So just as your hair starts to turn grey – which doesn't unduly worry you because you expect it to happen – you have forgotten over six million units – but your brain has stored up almost a million units you can recall. It is at this age we all start to worry about what we have forgotten instead of being astounded by what we can remember.

So instead of being delighted by the vast amount of facts you do remember, you start to worry about all the things you have been forgetting over the years. In truth, when you are sixty, you may forget your cousin's name, but you remember a tremendous amount of other facts.

We suggest that on some long winter evening you sit down with your spouse and discuss all of the facts you can recall about one specific year – for example the year that you met. Where you met, who you were with, your job at the time, where you lived, things you did together, everything that comes to mind. We bet that most women can remember the colour of the dress they were wearing when their future husband appeared.

You will be amazed how many units of information you can recall of that year – perhaps forty years ago. And don't worry if you cannot recall a few specifics. Remember, no one can recall more than 10% of what they have been exposed to.

We already can hear some of you saying, 'OK, I'll agree that I can recall events forty years ago. What worries me is that I often cannot remember what happened yesterday. Where did I leave my keys? What did Bill ask me to buy at the shops? Did I post that letter to my sister?'

This, too, is nothing new. All of us have forgotten a great deal of information we had absorbed as children. We are sure that every one of you can remember studying hard for an exam late into the night – and then, the next day, your mind being a complete blank on certain details that you thought had been permanently imprinted on your brain not twelve hours before.

In those days you did not worry that you might be becoming senile. You might have worried about what your parents were going to say if you failed, but that worry is no longer of concern. Also, you soon forgot almost everything you had so assiduously worked at remembering for that exam. And you were not unduly bothered.

We concluded the reason forgetfulness was a topic of more conversation in retirement marriages than it was in earlier life was that you now have more time to worry about things in general; and since most of your friends seem to be suffering with the same problem, it is convenient to discuss and to commiserate with each other over your supposed forgetfulness.

We recommend that you talk about it if you wish, but please do *not* worry about it. We are confident that each one of you has many more units of information in your brain than you have ever had; and that while you may forget certain things from time to time, this may be annoying to you, but it has nothing to do with your basic mental abilities.

AN EMBARRASSING PS FROM JOE

My own loss of memory recently put me into a most difficult situation. I have always claimed that when I forgot a person's name it was probably because I did not like him, or her, very much.

Over the years I have forgotten to go to two – yes, two – parties to which we were invited by someone of whom I was not particularly fond. I was expounding my theory about forgetfulness with a close friend and used as an example my forgetting these two parties – because I did not care for the hostess.

My good friend turned my face into a vivid shade of scarlet by saying, 'Joe, I invited you a party last January and you forgot to come.'

I no longer subscribe to my memory theory that forgetfulness comes from not liking a thing – *or a person*.

A RETIREE'S WIFE LAMENT.

The reason for much retirement sorrow
Is that he is here TODAY – and here TOMORROW.

39
Drink

... and why women make better alcoholics than men.

WHEN we started our interviews we were given a stern warning.

The warning was that men and women will respond with reasonable accuracy to many inquiries about their private lives – but never, ever rely on them telling the truth about sex or drink.

Extreme cases, however, are more dependable. The person whose sex life has always been a non-event will probably confess all. So will the out-and-out alcoholic – particularly if he or she has reformed. But those people who feel that perhaps they drink too much, or perhaps they perform less than brilliantly in bed, are not going to talk about it. Of course a few do, but most don't.

Maybe we struck lucky, but we both felt that the majority of our correspondents were quite honest about the drinking problem in retirement. Further, we were impressed by the number of wives who not only admitted to overdoing it, but also told us why they thought that they were better at 'getting away with it' than their husbands.

We must emphasize, of course, that women are *not* better at coping with alcohol on a physical basis. All medical evidence shows that men can drink more than women – sometimes much more – without suffering serious effects. The female body is not designed to take on board any excess of wine or spirits, particularly if it is short and slight. Unfortunate ladies have found themselves over the breathalyser limit after two modest glasses of sherry.

What emerged from our interviews was that women were good

secret drinkers; so good that even their husbands, who were home with them most days, did not realise what was going on.

The secret-boozing man acknowledged that he was usually caught out. He could hide bottles in the garden shed or the garage, but sooner or later his wife would come across them – and what possible excuse could he give for whisky among the spades and forks or behind an old tyre?

The wife, on the other hand, can have bottles galore in the kitchen; and if they are discovered, she can always claim they are for cooking. If she wants a secret nip at any time of day, she goes to the kitchen and the husband assumes she is just putting something in the oven. Frequent trips to the garden shed, or the garage, do not seem quite as natural or innocent, especially after dark.

Our impression was that wives were half sorry that they kept their secret so well. Kathleen T. wrote, 'Of course I don't want to be found out. Most of the time I am delighted that my husband hasn't a clue. But I do have this feeling that he ought to know. There's not much chance of sorting things out unless we do it together.'

Both men and women, who admitted to a drink problem, felt that retirement could make things worse; could even create the problem. One husband who has recently left his job told us, 'I honestly don't think my drinking was anything out of the ordinary while I was working but now, with little to do, I find myself in the pub more often. And I even treat myself to an occasional drink when I'm working in the garden.'

Doctors and professional advisers on alcohol abuse say, very definitely, that there comes a point when the drinker has to give it up – *altogether*! And if the drinking problem is of long standing, and appears to be getting worse rather than better, then we too would, reluctantly, have to agree.

We say 'reluctantly' because we both enjoy a periodic drink, and wine with our meals. (For many years Joe was Chairman of the International Wine & Food Society and he hates to think that fellow senior citizens should be deprived.)

If, however, the problem has started in, or made worse by, retirement, it is necessary to be aware of the warning signals. It might not be essential to take the drastic action of cutting alcohol out entirely, but it will take true character to keep the situation under control.

Some drastic action is needed – and soon. Kathleen T. is right to feel that her secret drinking – however successful – should come out into the open. This is not a 'NO-GO AREA' (Topic 30) where wives or husbands are entitled to their own privacy. It is an area where help from a married partner is truly needed. If the problem can be solved, this side of total abstinence, success could well depend on, as she said, '. . . sorting it out together'.

It is seldom easy to make confessions to one's nearest and dearest, so that's the hard part. That's the drastic action. Our other advice is relatively painless. Take a careful look at the topics in this book on health. Drinking problems often stem from the simple fact that you feel, not ill exactly, but under par. You want a booster, a happy-maker; and alcohol is one of the most available boosters around.

If you feel good anyway – where's the need? The enjoyment remains, but we would maintain that enjoyment is something different. It does not have to be excessive or addictive.

So we suggest that you try to give your health, your sense of well-being, a boost by other means. That's what our topics on health are all about.

You don't have to be told that 'Marriage Round the Clock' is going to be a whole lot more pleasant if it does *not* go along with 'Drinking Round the Clock', do you?

★ ★ ★ ★

TREE OF LIFE

An active, ardent gardening friend told her husband that she wanted a certain ornamental tree for her garden. Her husband came back in a few minutes and declared in no uncertain terms, 'I've looked it up in the book. You can't have it!'
She quietly enquired, 'Why not?'
His answer, 'You are 74, and it's a slow grower.'
'A joke', he thought.
'Not so funny', she thought.

★ ★ ★ ★

40
Optimism

Are you an optimist, a pessimist, or somewhere in between?

Dᴜʀɪɴɢ our interviews we talked with some out-and-out optimists, some obvious pessimists, and many others difficult to classify.

Rachael and Henry M. were certainly in the first category. They were both eighty and they had just planted a row of two-foot-high oak trees at the back of their garden. 'Several neighbours told us we were crazy,' Rachael said, 'but I tried to explain that both of us had a picture in our mind's eye of how the trees will look in a hundred years – and that is what we saw each time we looked at the saplings.'

Another couple in their sixties we found were both studying French even though they admitted that their finances would probably never allow them a holiday much more than 50 miles from their home in the Midlands. Their attitude was, 'You never know.'

André Simon, who founded the International Wine and Food Society, was an optimist all of his 93 years. He was working in England in 1914 when the First World War was declared. That very day, being a good Frenchman he decided to enlist in the French army, went to Victoria Station and brought a rail ticket to Paris. But the ticket he bought was a return ticket. He used the other half in 1919 on his return to England.

Further, when he was eighty, and one of the most famous men in the world of wine, he bought cases of fine Claret that would not be drinkable for ten more years and stored them in his cellar – and enjoyed them at their peak in his nineties.

André was an optimist, and his optimism made his long life an enjoyable one even though he had his share of life's tragedies – including being unemployed at the depths of the depression. His solution to this problem was to form the International Wine & Food Society and in so doing he gave great pleasure to tens of thousands of men and women around the world over the next fifty years.

It is often said that you have to be a little crazy to be an optimist throughout life. We do not disagree. But after talking with many couples we concluded that those couples where one partner or the other, or both, were that little bit crazy, and were optimists, enjoy their relationship much more than other couples who might be considered 100% sane. Many of the latter group tend to put the difficulties in life into much sharper focus in their minds than the delights.

It might be said that those couples who can be classified as being on the optimistic side have had less problems than their pessimistic counterparts. We cannot prove it, but we do not think this is true.

We classified as optimists some couples who have had serious health problems, financial problems, and even a variety of children and grandchildren problems. But their outlook was different and we came away convinced that their marriages and their entire life benefitted from their optimism.

Finally, on this subject, what about Martin and Marilyn H. – both in their late 70's? One of their many pleasures is going to the local hospital three mornings a week to entertain 'the old folks'. They thought it odd that we were interested in the fact that people their age would do this. They had never really taken time to think that they were technically 'old folks' themselves. They just said that they considered themselves optimists.

We recommend an optimistic view of life to one and all. We recognize that it is often difficult. Very difficult. But life can be impossible if you don't.

Optimism

A PS FROM PHOEBE

I have a woman friend who calls herself a pessimist. She denies that she is an optimist. However, I am not so sure. She explains that she is pessimistic because, by always expecting the worst to happen, she is agreeably surprised when it doesn't. What do you think she is?

41
Laughter

Sorry, but this is a sad subject.

An almost unanimous complaint we found in retirement marriages was that laughter no longer plays much of a part.

Time and time again we were told, 'When we were first married we used to laugh out loud often. I can remember on many occasions when I laughed so hard my sides ached. But for the last twenty years we have had very few belly laughs.'

There is, of course, a reason for this. You have heard every joke your mate knows time and time again. They were wildly funny the first time. But not the twenty-first time. Further, all of the highly amusing events of your life before marriage have been repeated many times. Also, the silly things that we used to do to make each other laugh now that we have grey hair unfortunately look undignified and do not engender laughter. More probably, a rebuke.

The lack of laughter is a common problem. If it troubles you and your partner you are in the company of many millions of married couples. When they stop to think about it, it troubles almost everybody.

What can be done about it?

We certainly wish that we had a definitive answer that would produce some hearty laughter in your home several times every day. But we don't have that answer.

The best we can do is to pass along a suggestion made by several couples who, over recent years, have been concerned that their laughter quota has fallen to such a low level.

They told us that the first thing they did was to have a little discussion on the subject, 'Where has our laughter gone?' Then they agreed to keep looking for things that might encourage laughter on the part of their mate. Snippets from the newspaper, an item from the radio, an amusing story picked up while having coffee with a friend.

They began to look for laughter-promoters from any source — and remembering them. They admit that they do not always succeed in generating anything more than a small smile; but every now and again they hit the jackpot and they both end up holding their sides. And when this happens it makes the whole exercise worthwhile.

Their final observation was that once they started to make a conscious effort to reintroduce laughter into their marriage, they themselves began to be more laughter prone.

One wife, who had been one of those who had suggested to us having a family discussion about the lack of laughter, told us that previously she could not remember laughing out loud for at least a whole year. But within two weeks after a discussion with her husband she found herself genuinely laughing out loud twice on one day.

She even laughed out loud as she was recounting to us the incidents that had so tickled her funny bone.

She was delighted. As was her husband. Because, as we all know, laughter is infectious. Their suggestion is worth a try.

A PS FROM PHOEBE

A former editor of *Punch* said that it was exceedingly difficult for him and his associates to sit around a table on a Monday morning and decide what, if anything, made the British people laugh.

One of their conclusions was that the funniest things were *not* intended to be funny. The editor cited a very serious article, in a very serious magazine, headed:

THE PLACE OF THE POTATO IN BRITISH FOLKLORE.

He thought that if any humorist tried to think up something as comical as that, he would fail.

My mother, a true English eccentric, was a superb illustration of the point. She never set out to be funny, but no one has ever made me genuinely laugh more. To take one of countless examples: she once went to an auction and accidentally bought a hundred lavatories. What really made me, and the whole family, laugh was the straight-faced way she reported the incident,

Yes, she reported, it had been a mistake, but she was absolutely certain they would all come in useful. Further, she said that she hadn't liked it when the auctioneer paused and asked, 'Madam, do you know what you're bidding for?' She considered it a gross impertinence.

The moral, perhaps, is that husbands and wives need not try to be great humorists in their own right. We can make each other laugh in other ways. Sometimes it is just a question of being very much yourself. (Like my mother.) But the safest approach, as mentioned earlier, is to try to remember any incident, any quote, which we know will appeal to our partner's sense of humour.

Old jokes, old stories can also be revived. Paul Y. wrote, 'Jill and I were in a restaurant celebrating our thirty-ninth wedding anniversary. We found ourselves remembering all the things that had made us laugh most in those thirty-nine years. And we started to laugh again. It came to be quite embarrassing. The other diners were looking around, wondering what had got into those two old codgers who were holding their sides, tears running down their cheeks, giggling like children.

'Certainly, we must do it again soon.'

★ ★ ★ ★

THE LEGAL APPROACH

There was a retired man from East Lyme
Who lived with three wives at one time.
When asked, 'Why the third?'
He replied, 'One's absurd,
And bigamy, Sir, is a crime.'

★ ★ ★ ★

42
Friends

. . . and is it back to childhood again?

I<small>N</small> the heady days of courtship there were likely to have been two very sobering experiences in your life. One was when you were told, 'I want you to meet my parents.' The other, 'I want you to meet my best friend.'

It's a daunting prospect, both for the boy and the girl, because you are so anxious to make a good impression – and you are aware that you may not succeed. You also wonder, 'What happens if I don't like them? Will it ruin everything?'

Now, here you are, still married all these years later, so presumably you were able to get by. (In spite of music hall jokes, many husbands and wives are genuinely fond of their 'in-laws'.) Further, as mentioned in our Introduction, mothers-in-law have probably vanished from the scene by now.

However, we found in our talks with older couples that the 'best friend', and indeed just regular friends of a husband or wife, can be a longer-lasting and more intractable problem. Friends are still here. If you have had the feeling that these pals of your partner are not the ones you would have chosen for yourself, time may have aggravated, rather than alleviated, your opinion.

Lady E., who married an officer in a prestigious British regiment, has never forgotten her engagement party. It was arranged so that each of them could meet the other's friends. The party was going well. That is until a Captain R., one of her future husband's closest friends, was introduced.

The Captain made no pretence at conversational congratulations. He bluntly stated, 'You're a damned lucky girl to get our Johnnie.' She was not pleased; but in those early days she felt she had to make an effort. If he was one of Johnnie's greatest friends, clearly she had to put up with him.

However, this tolerance did not last. Now she said, 'The man is such a *bore*. Always has been, always will be. I never have understood why Johnnie liked him. Although one accepts that a husband should keep his old friends, however dreadful they may be, there comes a time when you think, "Why should they be inflicted on me?" It would be better if they just had an occasional lunch together at the Club.'

As you might guess, this is also a subject on which husbands wax eloquent. In fact we came to believe they are even less tolerant than wives – and are often unprepared, at any stage of married life, to make much of an effort with their wife's friends whom they do not like.

A Ted N. is fairly typical. 'When I first met my wife's old friend, Daisy, I thought, "Here comes trouble." To begin with she looked like the back end of a bus; and, to go with it, she was a mischief-maker, always gossiping and stirring things up. I'm not very good at hiding my feelings and, right from the word go, my wife knew I didn't want her inflicted on me.'

When retirement comes, any couple is most unlucky not to have friends who are genuinely mutual; and most of these will have been acquired during their life together rather than inherited from their bachelor past.

You will, however, be lucky if all of your friends are shared; rather than having some who are liked by one partner and liked less – even actively disliked – by the other. We found only a handful of couples where this latter was not the case. So if you have the problem, you have lots of company.

Some compromise has to be right. Given the fact that most couples spend some time with other couples, there are bound to be niggles along the line. Mr. X likes Mrs. Y – but finds Mr. Y a bit of a buffoon. Perhaps Mrs. X agrees. Nevertheless, they are all old friends, get along pretty well, so they make allowances. (Of course, Mr. Y might also think Mr. X leaves a lot to be desired.)

Friends

We are sure that, come retirement, an arrangement has to be made. Separate get-togethers with old friends – whether your spouse likes them or not – should be part of life and certainly not a source of marital disagreement.

There are two important factors to be considered. First, before retirement, few people realize how big a part working colleagues played in their lives. They may not have been friends exactly; not people they wanted to have home for dinner or to join them on a holiday. All the same, it was a social, often stimulating, contact that has left a gap. So friends are needed more than ever to fill this gap.

Our correspondents made this point strongly; they even felt the need to re-establish contact with friends from way back who – perhaps because a spouse never liked them – have fallen by the wayside. Most likely, the spouse won't like them any more now than in the past, but that's not to say the friendship should never be resumed.

The second factor goes back to childhood. In our topic on *physical affection* we suggest that men, as they get older, revert to some habits of boyhood. (Embarrassment at displays of affection being one of them.) In the case of friends, we suspect that women, as well as men, can have something of a second childhood; again, nothing to do with senility. Just the resumption of a habit that seemed natural many decades ago.

It's the habit of preferring the company of people of your own sex; simply because they are more likely to be interested in the same things.

We are not suggesting that older couples cannot have common interests with other couples. It often happens. We are suggesting, however, that friends of one's own sex become more and more natural when we get older. As in childhood, we have more in common with them.

You can have a truly successful marriage without sharing every one of your friends. Now that you have more time for friends, it is most important to accept this basic fact – without resentment on either side.

The real mistake is to inflict someone too often on your partner when you know they do not get on. But neither should you be prepared to give up old friends. Neither partner has the right to expect this, however much they may object to the friend in question.

We are all for togetherness in marriage. But this is one area where husbands and wives should, at times, go their own way.

43
Role Reversal

What happens when a man retires, and a wife doesn't?

Our interviews found that this role reversal was not uncommon; partly because the wife was usually the younger partner – sometimes much younger – and also she has a feeling that her career was interrupted by children and, therefore, it ought to continue longer.

If she enjoys her job she could be reluctant indeed to quit. Jane C. admitted that she even invented reasons why she should keep working. 'I told Peter that we needed the money. I said it would be unfair to my boss who had been good to me. To be honest, neither of these things was really true. The fact was I just didn't want to sit at home all day. I knew it wasn't an important job. I am only a receptionist at a hotel and the pay isn't marvellous. But I liked meeting people, and the staff had become friends. I didn't want to give it up.'

Be warned. This can be a big bone of contention.

Quite often it seemed that the husband had made no objection. Not to begin with. He might treat it as a feminine whim; but if it kept her happy, why not? And perhaps the money would come in useful.

But few men who are still busy with full-time jobs can foresee what it will be like when he stays at home and she goes off to work. When that day comes he does not like it *at all*.

To begin with she would be less than human if she did not assume that he would take on some housewifely chores. What else has he got to do? Some shopping, some cleaning up, perhaps even some cooking. When she comes home and finds the place

157

pretty well as she left it, fur will fly. Surely he could have done something to help his hardworking wife.

But no, the husband doesn't see it like that.

Martyn G. wrote, 'When you retire you feel you have earned a bit of enjoyment and relaxation. I didn't retire to be a bloody cook, the way Joan seems to expect. I know she's a journalist, very good at her job, and I've never asked her to give it up. But she ought to see things from my point of view. We've always shared some of the chores but if she thinks she can come home, ask me to make her a drink, and then wait for me to dish up dinner, she can think again.'

We concluded that 'role reversal' in retirement comes harder that at other stages of married life. When a young man is out of a job, and the money earned by his wife is essential, he accepts the situation. He probably does not want to be a male housekeeper, but the young are adaptable. Moreover, he sees it all as temporary. He'll find another job and the natural state of affairs – man earning the daily bread, woman coping with home and family – will return.

The retired husband is far less likely to look at it that way. The wife's salary is often no longer essential, and Martyn G's reaction is typical. He has worked hard. He feels he has earned the right to a certain congenial lifestyle. And to be turned into a cook/housekeeper at his time of life is not congenial at all.

He goes on to report that the holidays he had long planned are being 'mucked about' because Joan is still working. He had set his heart on a leisurely trip abroad but Joan doesn't see how she can manage it. Not yet.

'And how long,' he asks, 'is not yet going on for? I could be in a wheelchair by the time she gets around to it. I'm healthy now and able to enjoy travel; but one has to be realistic. There aren't many years left and the time will come when I won't be able to cope with anything very adventurous. That's why I resent putting things off and off and off.'

So what do we say? There's the active, younger wife with a stimulating job; and there are wives who do not claim their work is 'important', but who still feel it is part of their life. Are they to give it up because their husbands dislike the role reversal?

Role Reversal

This may come as a surprise but we come down on the husband's side. (With, incidentally, Phoebe's enthusiastic support. While she thinks Martyn G. sounds a bit snappish and uncompromising, she feels he is right. He has earned the right to a congenial lifestyle – and his trip abroad. She feels it is hard to see how the marriage can become anything but sour if Joan frustrates him.)

It is not to say that the wife of a retired man must automatically become a devoted little homebody. (Who would dare suggest that to Mrs. Thatcher?) Other topics in this book stress the importance of stimulating projects for women as well as men and we will never go back on that.

Sometimes the project will involve a bit of role reversal; occasionally the man will have to be 'the bloody cook'. On an occasional basis there is nothing wrong with that.

We reckon, however, that the Mrs. Thatchers of this world have to be the exception. It is not much of a retirement marriage when the wife isn't available most of the week for running the home, for shared interests, for adventurous holidays.

We recognize that many wives may have to give up a lot; and husbands should not underestimate their need for out-of-the-household stimulus. Wives like Joan may find it difficult to adapt from a full-time job to more flexible arrangements.

But togetherness has to come first. And not many women can rely on having a husband like Dennis Thatcher

★ ★ ★ ★

TRY THIS ON FOR SIZE

'A king-sized bed is the invention of the devil' a 78-year-old correspondent wrote us. He claimed it provided too much room, and an older couple weren't forced into each others arms when they retired. He said that the ideal bed for a couple over 60 was a three-quarters bed. You had to hold onto each other all night to prevent falling out.

He urged us to see if our research could turn up an unhappy retired couple who slept in a three-quarter bed. He was willing to bet a fortune that we couldn't find one.

★ ★ ★ ★

44
Space

... and we don't mean outer space – the moon and the planets.

Most couples we talked to – and all experts in the field of retirement living – think that the amount of space in the home or flat is a most important factor in a successful marriage.

We heard many comments like, 'Jack is always underfoot now that he has retired' and 'Every time I want to be alone for a few minutes, Bill wanders in' and 'Just when I get my model-making tools out on the dining-room table to do some work, Henrietta tells me the neighbour is coming in for a cup of coffee.'

For these couples, space or, more importantly, the lack of it, is putting an additional strain on their marriages. We felt sorry for this group because they all thought that there was no solution to their problem. Or the only possible solution was to buy a larger house or flat – which in all cases was out of the question financially.

However, we found many other couples with what appeared to be an equally unsolvable space situation who did not consider space as one of their marriage problems.

For example, Joe S. and his wife Jane moved into a small terrace house the day he retired. (And we should add Joe is 6½ feet tall and Jane almost six feet. So there is a lot of them.) Joe loves to read – particularly history, and Jane does beautiful needlework for her family and friends. Jane likes to watch TV while she works so she uses an earphone so that it won't disturb Joe; and their small living room is so arranged that the flickering screen does not interrupt his concentration on the Spanish Armada.

Space

They did not consider their lack of space much of a problem. Nor did Bill P. His hobby is hooking rugs. In one corner of their living/dining room he has set up his loom with all materials close at hand. When he is working in what he calls his 'factory' – floor space exactly four feet by four feet – his wife Mildred can claim the whole remainder of the room for her activities.

We should add that Mildred willingly agreed to have her friends in for a cup of coffee without making Joe dismantle his loom. She figured that she really did not enjoy the company of anyone who would object to a loom in the living room.

One American couple, a retired doctor who loved to play the viola, solved their problem by deciding that space was more important than the paint on their automobile. So they leave their car outside and have converted their small garage into a music studio where he can practise to his heart's content.

However, they did report a bit of a minor problem because one viola player in a garage did not take up much space – much less than a motorcar – and they began to use the extra area for storing things. Before the viola player was forced back to the living room, because of lack of enough room to move his playing arm, they jointly made the decision that every inch of space needed for a car would be left free for the musician.

These couples, and many others, thought we were kidding them when we asked if they needed more space to make their marriage work. Some of them had other problems, but this was not one of them. (A friend of ours reported that recently she was on an aeroplane and the 64-year-old woman sitting next to her admitted that she was leaving her recently retired husband. Our friend asked why. Her answer was, 'We live in a big house but my husband insisted on doing everything in the kitchen – including giving me constant advice on my cooking.' She had had enough.)

However, space problems, like most other problems, can be solved by forthright discussion between the partners. Often we found that when lack of space bothered one partner, the other was not aware there was a problem. As Henrietta, whose model-making husband was upset by having to move his kit, told us, 'I never thought it bothered Joe to move it. He always seemed to get pleasure out of shuffling his things about. From now on he can leave it there all day.'

So, if you do have a space problem, we suggest you work it out together. We talked with so many couples who have solved the problem – even one pair who lived in a single room, studio flat – that we know solutions can be found.

It all comes down to respecting the need for his, or her, space – that is, after finding out what his or her space needs to be.

★ ★ ★ ★

FOR BETTER OR FOR WORSE

We talked with a couple from Wales who had recently celebrated their Golden Wedding – by buying themselves a new double bed. (Previously having had singles.)

The husband observed that we all have heard, 'Families who pray together, stay together,' But he thought, equally important, was 'Couples who sleep together, keep together.'

★ ★ ★ ★

45
Living Habits

Are you an 'average' retired couple?

IN order to give us background information on retired couples we made an informal survey and asked them to tell us how they lived each day.

While we cannot assure you that our survey results are as precise as those claimed by political pollsters, the replies certainly indicate that there was no one pattern of living. There seemed to be as many patterns as there were respondents.

For example, the question, 'How often do you have breakfast together?' produced these answers:

70% usually breakfast together.
20% occasionally breakfast together.
10% seldom, if ever, breakfast together.

When it came to lunch:

40% usually lunch together.
50% occasionally lunch together.
10% seldom lunch together.

(Note – two couples reported that they *never* have breakfast *or* lunch together. We never were able to determine why.)

We asked, 'Do you ever read newspapers or watch TV while dining?'

10% very often read during meals.
30% occasionally read during meals.
60% claim they never read during meals.

As for TV:

> 40% do watch TV during meals. (Mainly the news.)
> 40% occasionally watch TV during meals.
> 20% were adamant that they never watched TV.

(Personal observations on the value of reading or watching TV at meals will be found in our topic titled MEAL HABITS.)

Next we enquired about the amount of travel each couple took the previous year. To make the answers more specific we asked how many nights they spent away from their home during the period. The answers varied from zero to 150. Yes, one couple spent five months travelling.

The rough average was about 30 days; but that included visits to the homes of children – probably to baby-sit with the grand-children. Most couples, by the time of retirement, more or less agreed on the importance of travel in their lives. However, 20% of the wives liked to travel much more than their husbands; and another 10% of the husbands admitted they liked to travel more than their wives.

As to sleeping arrangements:

> 50% slept in a double bed (king size, queen, or regular).
> 30% in twin beds
> 20% usually slept in separate rooms, (almost all of these mentioned the word 'snoring').

We were interested in whether retired husbands made much of a contribution in the kitchen. And we found:

> 55% never take the responsibility for the main meal.
> 30% of all husbands occasionally prepare the entire main meal.
> 10% claim to cook the main meal at least once a week.
> 5% do most of the cooking. (A wife's illness is a factor here.)

As to washing up:

> 30% did all, or at least most, of the washing up.
> 65% helped wash up most of the time.
> 5% never washed or dried or even put a dirty dish in a machine.

(Note from Joe. I sure would like to know how the 5% managed this.)

Finally we asked a difficult question. 'When you two are alone at a meal how much of the time do you talk with each other?'

> 45% indicated that they talked almost continuously (if they were not reading or watching TV at the time).
> 40% said they talked to each other about half of the time.
> 15% reported conversation somewhat less than half the time.

However, in that bottom 15% of communicators we found happily married couples who told us they usually talked very little – including two – who said, 'We often sit through a whole meal without saying a word.'

The obvious conclusion from these, and other questions, is that no two retired couples live precisely the same way. Therefore, no one should ever worry if their living habits seem to be at odds with a friend's or a neighbour's.

Your marriage may be among the majority where the husband helps wash up but you may be with the minority in seldom having breakfast together. So what? If this is the living arrangement you two prefer, stay with it.

We have become convinced that there is no such thing as an 'average' retirement marriage. And we are not sure we would recommend it even if there was.

46
Boredom

Is it a factor in retirement marriages?

I N truth, after all of our interviews we could not determine whether boredom was a factor that concerned many couples.

However, we believe there is a good reason why we had so much difficulty in trying to throw light on what we called 'the boredom enigma'. And the reason is that it is almost a cliché with retired men to claim, 'I've never been busier in my life. There are hundreds of things I would like to do but have not had time for.'

On the other side of the coin, wives told us over and over again, 'Bored? I don't have time to be bored. Now that my husband is around all day I have to work much harder than I ever did. I'd even welcome a few quiet minutes of boredom every day.'

So many respondents were so positive with statements such as these we began to suspect that retirement boredom might indeed be a problem. To paraphrase Shakespeare, 'Methinks thou doth protest too much.'

Our friend Brian W., for the last ten years of his business career, kept saying, 'When I retire I am going to pursue boredom. I've heard about boredom all my life, and I want to see what it is like.' And, in a way, Brian meant it.

But he has now been retired over five years and as we see him from time to time we know he really is engaged in so many genuine activities that he has not yet achieved his goal of comprehending boredom. It may be that Brian, and many other retired men, have such an ingrained dislike of boredom – even the possibility of being bored – that they do everything they can to make sure they don't catch the disease.

Boredom

Even going so far as to not quite telling the truth when questioned on the subject lest they become infected.

At the end of our research we concluded that there are almost as many different strains of the boredom disease as there are of the flu disease. On the one hand some boredom strains are fatal – while on the other hand some strains are so mild that the victim is never inconvenienced, much less sick.

We found that men who were often bored during their working life usually suffered attacks of boredom after retirement. However, there were some major exceptions to this finding. Joe L. was one of these. He told us, 'For thirty years I worked on the assembly line in the motorcar industry doing exactly the same thing for months, sometimes years, on end. Everyone agreed it was a boring job. From the day I retired and could potter in the garden or fool around in my workshop or go to the pub at 11am – whatever, I have never felt that same kind of tedious boredom. And it's been seven years.'

On the other hand men who had had a relatively exciting working life seem to continue to be stimulated, and not bored, after retirement. The exception with this group appeared to be a few passive-by-nature men who happened, by chance, to have worked surrounded by active, vital associates who kept their laid-back comrades from being bored while working at their job. In retirement, when they were on their own, they succumbed to fits of boredom.

From a wife's angle, Gretchen D.'s comment tells the whole story. 'I worked until I was sixty. Then I retired. But it is now fifteen years later and I have not been able to retire from my job of being a wife. Men retire. Working women retire. But wives don't retire. Of course there are many things I would like to do now – but can't for various reasons. But as for boredom, I am no more bored now than I was during my combined working and being-a-wife years. I think women can handle it better. Perhaps, because, as I said, wives don't retire.'

The final, and very sad, point about the boredom disease is that no doctor can cure it; no psychiatrist can cure it; no one can cure it except the victim himself or herself. Outside people may help a little but the real cure comes directly from the victim.

From our observations there is a boredom factor in some marriages, in spite of the plethora of protests. Some men and some women have cured themselves, or at least put the disease into remission.

So, it can be done. But it's up to you.

A PS FROM JOE

Many years ago a psychologist friend of mine told me in all seriousness that a person should not trouble seeing a psychiatrist, or a psychologist, if they were happy more than *fifteen minutes a month*. He explained that there were so many people who did not have fifteen minutes of happiness in a thirty day period that they should have first priority in seeking professional help.

This has troubled me for years. Even if my friend were exaggerating and the true figures were, let's say, less than fifteen minutes of happiness a day for some unfortunate people, I have felt extremely sorry for them.

The good news – at least I think it is good news – is that he did not classify being bored as, necessarily, being unhappy. His classification – albeit very oversimplified – of human experience was as follows:

Category A – Happiness, delight, laughter, pleasure, joy, ecstasy, rapture.

Category B – The daily chores (peeling potatoes, shaving, Hoovering, watching most TV, driving to work, etc.), dullness, drabness, monotony, and simple boredom.

Category C – Tragedy, despair, unhappiness, misfortune, grief.

Even if you are bored occasionally that is a whole lot better than being in Category C – where, believe it or not, some unfortunate people are imprisoned almost all of their time.

My psychologist friend, while he recognizes that we all have to spend much time in Category B, insists that we all have it in ourselves to reach Category A on occasion.

However, he agrees that there is only one person who can manage to get you there.

You.

47
Money

. . . and when should a retired couple start to spend
some of their capital?

EVERY marriage has, in one degree or another, some problem
with money.

This came as no surprise to us because we had reasoned that
money always is a problem – particularly as it always seems
everybody would like to have more money than they do.

But what did come as a surprise was that the lack of what
people considered 'enough money' was only one of many problems that money engendered in retirement marriages. For
example, one couple, both in their early 70's, told us they
thought that they had enough money to live comfortably for the
rest of their lives, but they could not bring themselves to spend
even the money they had coming in because for 45 years they
had always put some aside each month into savings 'for a rainy
day'.

They had had a few financial rainy days during their married
life and this policy had been of help to them. But now the habit
was so ingrained they couldn't stop it even though they both
agreed that occasionally they would like to go out to an extrava-
gant lunch, or take a vacation, or buy a new colour TV to replace
their 15-year-old one.

What might be viewed as the amusing problem was that from
time to time Jane, the wife, would suggest that they spend some
of their savings, but Herman would always drag his feet. A
month or so later it would be Herman who suggested a minor
luxury, but Jane put her foot down. Both seemed to take turns in
being over-cautious. Further, they both told us that their four

children would certainly help financially if they really ran into a serious problem.

Of course, we often encountered the problem where the wife, or the husband, thought that the other was spending too much of their income – and the income was almost always less than they enjoyed before retirement. Interestingly, the complaints about overspending were almost equally divided between husbands and wives.

Another situation was typified by Miriam S. who reported that over the years her husband's salary represented over 90% of the family income. She had only occasional part-time jobs while raising the family. But Miriam said, 'When Bill was working he always considered my contribution to our finances equal to his. There was never any problem about the money we spent being "his" money. It was always "our" money. But now he keeps pointing out to me that all the money we have comes from *his* pension, *his* savings, even *his* Social Security. Technically he is correct. But it upsets me. Why did his attitude change when he retired?'

Our only answer to Miriam and other wives who raised the question was that when a man retires he recognizes that there will be no more rises (other than index-linked ones) and if he wants to maintain in his mind that he is still the breadwinner of the family, he goes overboard in claiming the credit for all the family income. Not much of an answer, perhaps, but it seems to be the truth.

One common denominator in all our research was that regardless of the amount of income or capital that a couple has they become increasingly cautious with age. We would like to have taken many of the couples we interviewed by the scruff of the neck and shaken them up and told them they should spend more of their annual income, whatever it was, and do some little extra things that would give them both pleasure.

When we asked, 'What are you saving it for?' the answer was usually 'Well, let me think.' Then they would be hard put to it to come up with a logical answer. Many times it was, 'We might have an expensive illness.' Yes, that is a possibility, but we were amazed at the number of couples that were in their 80's who haven't had a major costly illness. (It could be that these couples did spend a little more on some comforts or luxury, like a nice vacation, when they were in their 70's and thereby avoided an illness.)

Finally we tried to find out what couples thought was the ideal annual income for a retired man and wife. The answer reminded us of a survey Dr. Gallup did many years ago when he found that the average wage earner thought that 20% more than whatever he was earning would solve all of his financial problems. We sensed that almost all those we interviewed would agree they would have no problems with just 20% more income.

We have thought long and hard after our many talks about money with retired couples and we have tried to develop some thoughts that might be helpful.

Our first conclusion was that there are many, many couples who would like to spend a bit more to buy something they want for their home, or for travel, or for whatever – but are too cautious to do it – who will die with too much money in their estate. A well-known financial adviser tells his clients, 'Go first class. Your heirs will.'

He obviously does not mean that you should necessarily fly first class. What he is saying is that you should treat yourself to a little more than you think you can afford. You've earned it. Enjoy it.

A PS FROM PHOEBE

It is not only concern about money which afflicts people as they get older. (And as we have pointed out, these concerns can often be irrational.)

There are two other points I think should should be stressed. In our topic on ECCENTRICS we mention that people could become more eccentric as they get older; and this statement can be enlarged. Our strongest characteristics, good or bad, tend to become more pronounced with age. If we are naturally frank, we become franker. If we are naturally generous, we become more so. If we are naturally mean, we become meaner.

Money can be a very sore point between husband and wife.

When one partner is definitely stingy, the other hates it. And if they get stingier than ever in retirement, all hell can break loose. As a rule the man still controls the finances; so I am personally warning him to *watch it*. A young husband can argue that he is saving for the children, for the future. An old miser who pinches for no good reason on the housekeeping has nothing to recommend him at all.

My second point, seen from the wife's side, has to do with inflation. A woman, who does the daily shopping, is obliged to keep abreast of it. (More or less.) The man may have the odd fit of hysterics when the electricity bill comes in; but price rises on the countless items that go into the daily shopping basket are not so much a part of his life.

He can be honestly baffled by the question, 'Where does all the money go?' He reads about inflation in the newspapers, but somehow it does not translate into facts like, 'Bread cost 10p a few years ago – 60p now.'

The only real solution is to take your husband shopping with you occasionally. This may not be practical when he is in a full-time job but it certainly can be done now that he is retired.

If you have a mate who has been inflation-proof, I recommend it.

★ ★ ★ ★

CONVERSATION PIECE

We learned about one retired man who had married a luscious 29-year-old several years before he had retired.
We also learned that he recently had taken on a mistress – a 64-year-old widow he had met at a party.
His explanation – that he had to have some one he could talk with.

★ ★ ★ ★

48

Sports

Are you part of the 50% who regularly indulge?

OR are you in that other 50% that considers yourself too old for sporting activity? If so, read on.

Our interviews and questionnaires turned up the surprising fact, at least to us, that just over 50% of older couples regularly involve themselves in one sport or another. This was good news.

Now, we don't mean sports like football and rugby – but rather swimming, tennis, bowls, golf, bicycling, jogging, hiking, etc. and etc.

(But we did talk to one 70-year-old marathon runner, and two 80-year-olds who could skip rope as well as an exuberant 10-year-old. And one 65-year-old slow bowler who had taken two wickets at a recent village cricket match. Further, he was a little upset because if his grandson hadn't dropped two easy catches, he would have had four wickets.)

This sporting endeavour was good news to us. This is because there is a growing realization among medical experts that sports and exercise are of vital importance in keeping older people in better health, both physical and mental.

As one doctor advised us, 'If I could give many of my patients a bicycle, and convince them to go for a short ride each day, my prescriptions for pills would drop immediately.' He went on to say that the medical world does not want men and women over 60 trying to run a four-minute mile, climb Mt. Everest, or jog from Land's End to John O'Groats.

What doctors would love to see is everyone in our age group, who is in satisfactory health to begin with, doing some relatively

simple sport or exercise every day. If nothing more than brisk walking – not just strolling – a mile or two on as many days a week as possible.

In the United States, particularly in the northern parts where the weather prevents much outdoor activity during the long winter, more and more doctors have convinced their older patients to buy a stationary bicycle – and to pedal it for twenty or thirty minutes every day.

This is not as painful as it sounds. Many of these bicycles can be positioned in a house so that the rider can watch TV while churning up his daily quota of 'miles'. Others are equipped with a device that holds a book, so if reading is preferred to TV, it is easily done.

Doctors there recognize that such a piece of equipment costs a substantial amount of money, but they point out the cost is less than for a room for half a day's stay in a hospital – and the healthy exercise the owner secures should prevent, they say, at the very least, that amount of saving. (Of course, in the UK if you are on NHS, you would not save any hospital costs but few people look forward to being in hospital.)

However, what interested us even more in discussions with the medical fraternity, was the fact that some daily exercise improves a person's mental outlook as much, if not more, than their physical well-being. So it can be said that exercise makes your healthier and happier at the same time.

Another important aspect to sports and exercise for an older couple is the fact that they can often do it *together*. Husbands and wives usually have some separate interests – and that's fine. But they should also have some mutual ones that they can share together. And that's where sports and exercise offer a golden opportunity.

Don and Helen D. took up bowls after he retired. 'I didn't do any exercise at all until then,' he said, 'and bowling is not the most wildly active sport. However, since we started five years ago I am convinced I feel much better, and so does Helen. When the weather is good we often spend a whole afternoon at our little club.'

Another bowls player, who also agreed that the sport was not taxing, reported that he and his wife not only play together, but also walk the mile and half to their club, and home again. 'By walking briskly we can do it in twenty-five minutes. We stroll home in thirty. But the whole experience is stimulating,' they said.

So many outdoor sports in the UK are controlled by the weather – but various couples mentioned that they do their best not to let the vagaries of the British climate interfer with their exercise. 'On holiday, when it is too cold to go swimming,' Eugene Z. told us, 'we bundle up and walk. We even like it in the rain.'

We found some couples who could force themselves to do calisthenics at home – a form of exercise neither of us fancy.

However, they reported unanimously that their daily gyrations, lying on the bedroom floor, were of great benefit to them.

Concerning sports and exercise, we ended up with one regret. Namely, that there is so little publicity in the press or on TV about older sports enthusiasts, and how truly enthusiastic they are about what it does for them.

If a famous footballer has a small pain in his stomach, or a well-known runner stubs his toe, or a professional golfer has a cold, we hear about it *ad nauseum*.

But when an eighty-year-old couple play three sets of tennis, singles, most days; or others take a holiday in the winter, to go cross country skiing; or still others hike around the entire coast of Cornwall in March; we don't hear about it.

If these activities, and many others, were known, more and more older couples would be encouraged to emulate them. And would feel much better for doing so.

And when an 85-year-old couple quietly walk five miles every day, rain or shine, near their village in Shropshire, it seldom makes news.

It should.

But it certainly makes them feel better and, we believe, makes their marriage a much happier one.

★ ★ ★ ★

A QUINTESSENTIAL QUARTET

'I've always thought you need four husbands. One who smokes a pipe and is cosy in front of a fireplace. One who is good at conversation. One who is good at getting to the top of queues and finding taxis. And one who is good at sex.

'Now that we're retired, I need the four more than ever.'

Hazel West

49
The Telephone

. . . and what's the answer to the answering problem?

Who would have thought that we would have found something as basic as the telephone a problem in many long-
term marriages?

It came as a complete surprise to us. We thought that after
sharing a bed for many years, sharing a telephone would cause
no problems at all.

But we were wrong.

First of all, who answers it when both of you are at home?
During the working years it was easy. Either the children picked
it up, or usually one of the parents was out of the home. So the
question of who should answer it never came up.

But now it is different. We found in many homes either the
husband or the wife is almost always charged with answering the
phone. And what's important is that in many cases the answerer
resents that he or she is lumbered with this responsibility.

Our figures indicated that the answering was done by the man
in 80% of the homes. 20% by the wives. Interestingly, if we can
believe our figures, 80% of the calls were for the wife, 20% for
the husband.

Further, the telephone problem as reported to us does not end
there. Another area of contention is the length of many calls.
The complainers are mostly, as you might guess, the husbands.
As one told us, 'My wife spends half the day on the telephone
and then says she hasn't time to do something else.' We are
certain he was exaggerating. We think that most husbands say
they are concerned about the time they thought that their wife

177

was wasting on the telephone, while the real reason for their concern is the telephone bills they will have to pay later on.

Yet another area where the telephone featured in occasional family discord was not limited to one sex or the other. Evidently, this problem develops in almost every home, with both husbands and wives, and it ignites an immediate and wild fury in the person talking on the phone at the time.

We are sure you recognize the situation. The person on the telephone is in mid-sentence, and the spouse from across the room shouts, 'Find out if Bill got that book I sent him!' or 'Ask Charlie if Miriam's cousin is really going to marry that lazy lout.'

What happens? The one on the telephone doesn't comprehend the shouted question, the person on the other end of the line hears incomprehensible confusion in the background, and then a cross, 'Hold on a minute, Jim is trying to say something to me.'

For the next thirty seconds no one knows who is talking, the thread of the interrupted conversation has long since been lost, a small family insurrection has been started, and in the end no one really knows whether the book has been received or Miriam's cousin has succumbed to the impoverished lout.

We concluded that everyone is occasionally guilty of this crime – including ourselves. We are determined that from now on when we wish to interject a thought or a question into a telephone conversation, we will quietly get out of our chair, walk across the room, gently touch the talker on the shoulder, raise a finger to indicate that before he or she hangs up we would like to make a statement, and then patiently stand by to be recognized.

Of course, after standing there for a few minutes we will probably have forgotten what we wanted to say. But does that really matter? Most shouted-across-a-room queries are not all that vital. Besides we can always ring back.

This is not much of a solution. The only better one is to swear you will never, never, never interrupt a running telephone conversation. But this is an impossible dream. It is so easy to interrupt and we are sure that we will be halfway into our shouted question before we remember our resolve.

So if you decide to try this latter plan, good luck.

The Telephone

A final note on the telephone. We found a few people – both men and women – who can let the telephone ring and ring and ring – and not answer it. Even here we uncovered a telephone-related irritation because there were no homes where both partners could resist the siren's call of a ringing telephone. In the end, it always happens, one or the other shrieks, 'Damn it – I'll answer the ——— thing.'

To make matters worse, when answered, the caller wants to speak to the other spouse, with some information he or she has been waiting for for days.

So we had all better learn to live with the telephone. We can't live without it. Or can we?

50
Letters

. . . and can they help your retirement marriage?

'LETTERS – personal letters – played a large role in making our marriage a pleasant one,' reported one of our interviewees. The wife was confined to a wheelchair much of the time. The husband had lost a leg in the war and had difficulties hobbling around. He had been retired as a watch repair man for three years.

Her story continued. 'We found that after my husband retired we were spending more and more time alone in the house. Because of our health problems we had great difficulty getting out and seeing people. In truth we were getting lonely. Then, one day, for some reason I decided to write a letter to my niece in Scotland. A week or so later we received a nice note from her and in it she mentioned her brother had recently moved to Cornwall.

'Now, I was never much of a letter writer – and I'm still not – but I wrote him a letter asking about his new life and soon received a most interesting answer. Incidentally we still correspond about once a month. And I have never seen him since he was seven and now he has five children. But no matter.

'On a rainy day I took a chance and wrote to a woman I grew up with. She only lives twenty miles away and we hadn't seen each other for years. I found she too couldn't get around very well but she writes long letters about the things she is doing, TV shows she's enjoyed, and we reminisce about our life a long time ago.'

It turned out that this couple – the husband has also started writing letters to old army friends – are in touch by post with almost thirty different people, including a distant relative in Kenya, and a friend who emigrated to Australia.

It was obvious in talking with this pair that their life had taken on a new meaning since they started to put pen to paper. Their eyes sparkled when they read us excerpts from a letter from another niece's son who was a student in University in Texas. From a health standpoint this couple had more than their share of problems, but as the wife stated emphatically, 'We're not lonely any longer.'

Oh yes, we have to say that they had also written to other people but had not received any replies from them. It seems some people just cannot bring themselves to write letters. Our couple thought that this was sad but they had found enough correspondents to keep their minds busy and their life interesting and they just had to forget about these non-letter-writers.

We found other couples who complained, 'Nobody ever writes to us.' However, in each case when they were asked how many letters they had written recently, the answer was none.

It is an indisputable fact that the amount of letters a person receives is in direct relation to the number written.

Practically everyone enjoys receiving letters (other than bills) and for many retired couples the arrival of the post is one of the highlights of the day. Further, one of the interesting things we discovered in discussing letters with our interviewees was that the pleasure of receiving a letter had nothing to do with the length of a letter, nor the literary quality, nor even the accuracy of the spelling – but rather from the fact that a friend had sat down for a few minutes, put some words to paper, and, in so doing, thought about you.

So we suggest you think of some friend – even an acquaintance – or, for that matter, a relative – whom you have not seen for a long time and write them a letter. The odds are that in short order you will receive one from them. And, in due course, answer that letter. You will find it much less difficult to write a reply than the opening letter. Expert letter writers tell us that it is much easier to write someone every day than it is to write every month. We do not recommend writing every day, but we do enthusiastically suggest writing to at least one person every day. It will add an interesting dimension to your life.

Final suggestion. We all like to receive positive, enthusiastic letters – not one about someone else's aches and pains. At our age we have enough of our own. So when you write, tell about what your grandchildren are up to, or about a walk in the woods on a fine autumn day, or a TV show, or a book you have read, or a delicious plum tart your wife has made.

There is a direct relationship between letter writing and conversation. If you see someone every day you have lots to talk about; if you see them once a month the conversation is less fluent; and with someone you see only once a year it takes much longer to get up a conversational head of steam. So the more often you write, the easier it becomes.

Try it. Start now and think of a friend you would like to hear from. All it takes after you made that decision is a pen, some paper, and you are off. Dear ———.

A PS FROM JOE

A younger friend of ours – a man – has parents living in a nursing home who are not in good health. Our friend – their only child – has made it a point for several years to drive the 90 miles – and 90 more back – every week to visit his parents for an hour or so. Spending time, and money, he can ill afford.

Recently he asked his parents, 'Do you want me to continue these visits?' Their surprising answer – given with a little embarrassing hesitation – was, 'Yes, we do like seeing you. But could you write us a letter from time to time? We can read your letters over and over again – which we enjoy. While when your visit is over we have nothing until you next appear.'

So now he writes letters – often short ones – just reporting what he and his wife have been doing. And now his parents write back. Everyone is pleased. (He still visits them once a month or so.)

For the investment of an hour a week (rather than the six or seven previously); a few stamps (which cost rather less than eight gallons of petrol) – has resulted in a wonderfully satisfying arrangement all round.

A letter is a very valuable experience – for both parties.

TIMELESS

The former American President, Jimmy Carter, admitted to having 'unreasonable standards' about punctuality. If Rosalyn were even a few minutes late there would be a furious exchange, '. . . and we would arrive at Church or a friend's house still angry with each other. For 38 years it has been the most persistent cause of dissension between us.'

One morning, Jimmy suddenly realised that it was his wife's birthday and he did not have a gift.

But he had brilliant idea. He wrote a note. 'HAPPY BIRTHDAY. As proof of my love I will never again make an unpleasant comment about tardiness.' The note was delivered with a kiss.

This happened in 1982 and he is still keeping his promise. Both agree that it was the best birthday present he had ever given her.

51
Courtesy

Should you still stand up when a woman, your wife, enters the room?

COURTESY, it is often said, is only noticed when it is neglected. And we found courtesy neglected in rather more marriages than we expected. Including, when we started to analyse it, and we regret to report this, in both of our own. We, like many others, had let ourselves take courtesy for granted. (Ted and Audrey, we apologize.)

Most marriages we sensed said 'Please' and 'Thank you' to each other often enough. Though one delightfully dignified eighty-five-year old philosophized to us, 'It is impossible to say those two words too often.'

Such basic courtesy, we found, was not a problem with most marriages. However, we did uncover various critical observations and complaints when we asked individuals, in private conversations, 'Is your husband – or wife – as courteous to you now as he – or she – was on your honeymoon?'

In almost every case, after a moment's hesitation, we received the answer, albeit a somewhat guarded one, 'No, I don't think so.'

Sonia B.'s comment was typical of many. 'When Gordon and I first went out, before we were married, he never failed to open the car door for me. And he always had an umbrella handy if there was a spot of rain. But some place along the line, probably when the children were small and it took both of us to get the family aboard, he must have stopped the door-opening, and umbrella, courtesy. I didn't notice it for years but now that there is just the two of us, I have to admit I miss it and I wish he would do it again.'

Husbands had their share of complaints too. Listen to Max F's grumble. 'Just after the war, when we were first married, and I took Helen out to see a movie and perhaps a drink at the pub, she would thank me for a wonderful evening when we got home and then again, just as enthusiastically, the next morning. Now, forty years later, if I take her out for a fancy dinner the most I get from her is a "It was nice", and that's the end of it.'

By tradition it would seem that the male of the species has more opportunities to perform the obvious courtesies – holding a woman's coat when she is putting it on, opening car doors, actually opening all doors and letting the woman through first, or holding a chair when she sits down.

In past years a man could tip his hat, and even remove it in a lift when there was a woman present, but this courtesy is now seldom exercised as so few men wear hats.

THEN...   NOW...

The courtesies that the female of the species are expected to extend to her mate are more subtle – other than producing enough enthusiastic 'thank you's' when the occasion demands.

Many husbands did praise their wives for what we called out-of-the-immediate-family courtesies. They remembered your Aunt Emma's birthday, and they would telephone, or write a note, to thank a friend for a dinner or some favour.

And wives still do bring their husband's slippers after he has shed his Wellingtons following several hours' work in the garden in a driving rain. They even bring a cup of steaming hot tea. As Bill D. told us in emphatic terms, 'That's courteous, even though not one courteous word has been spoken.'

Our conclusion after all these discussions on courtesy was that it, like many other habits, merely depended on our being aware of the need for, and the opportunity for, little bits of courtesy. No one we talked with had ever made a conscious decision to be less courteous. It was merely a case of the subject slowly slipping from the mind over the years.

Courtesy is important. Don't let it slip yours.

A PS FROM BOTH PHOEBE AND JOE

We cannot conclude this topic concerning COURTESY, or politeness, without mentioning our topic on MARITAL ENCOURAGEMENT. All of our interviewees agreed that there is a big difference between being courteous, and being encouraging, to your partner. They are two distinctly different subjects. Each plays a leading role in a pleasant marriage.

★ ★ ★ ★

WE'LL TAKE THIS FOR GRANTED

'I didn't like it when my husband took me for granted when I was twenty.
Now that I am eighty, I like it even less.'

Susan Hatch

★ ★ ★ ★

52

A Party Game

. . . and one that might help a marriage. Really?

Nₒᴛ everyone enjoys party games; and they don't always contribute to marital harmony. (Phoebe reports that she found it hard to forgive her husband Ted, when once, after a game of charades with friends, he commented when they got home, 'You certainly made a right fool of yourself acting out "The Virgin Birth".' Phoebe admits he was right; and that made matters worse.)

There is also a feeling that after 'a certain age' we all tend to think of party games as childish. It is an easy rationalization.

However, we came upon a game which many players thought was entertaining; and, further, it exercised the minds of couples – especially older couples – in a way that was entirely constructive. Unlike "The Virgin Birth" episode, the couples went home feeling pleased with each other. Pleased and flattered.

Here is the game.

You have to imagine that your spouse is up for sale, and you have to write a short advertisement to attract prospective purchasers. You are hoping to get the best possible price, so he or she must be presented in the most attractive possible light. At the same time, you have to be realistic and anyone describing an unrecognizable picture of their partner is disqualified.

So, what do you do? We found that young couples can dash off something quite easily. Their advertments talk a lot about looks and sex appeal. Older couples take longer, think harder. When you are putting a 65-year-old up for sale, you can't be glib about it. The fact that you've been married to this 'property' for many years makes you concentrate on the enduring qualities.

For example, humour will feature more in the ads than bust measurements. Kindness rather more than tailoring. It is a bit difficult because, as many retired couples tell us, one of their common problems is that their partner 'just takes me for granted'. Neither side stops to think what makes the husband or wife 'a desirable sale'.

Here are a few examples:

FOR SALE. 66-year-old male who can make you laugh when the dishwasher breaks down – just after Christmas dinner; when the electricity is cut off because you had forgotten to pay the bill; or when you have to walk after the car runs out of petrol a mile from home. Fine head of silver hair which should last forever. Bit of a paunch, but stable. Unconversational after dinner, possibly asleep; but very good-tempered at breakfast. Exceptionally nice to elderly ladies.

BARGAIN OFFER. Woman whose complexion is rose and cream – although at her age she has no right to it. Very soft cheeks. Nice to nuzzle. Loses her temper about once a week but never sulks. Lovely bedside manner when man is ill. And in other circumstances.

COSY PIPE-SMOKING MALE AVAILABLE. Not very anxious to take you to the theatre, ballet, or opera – but an outstanding gardener. Deep, gentle speaking voice, easy on the ear even when he's cross. Which is seldom. No hair to speak of but gorgeous dark eyes. Like Guinness.

SALE CANCELLED. Offer of a 74-year-old female, with assorted faults, has been withdrawn. Her husband has concluded that he could not possibly live without her for a single day.

When played in a group – each contestant, after 15 minutes of writing, reads his advertisement to all the others – or husbands and wives can exchange their ads so that the person 'for sale' reads the copy his spouse thinks will 'sell' him or her.

The game will produce considerable hilarity – but, more

importantly, will give long-married couples the opportunity to think about what a good 'product' they are married to – when the advertisement they write, like all advertisements, concentrates on the positive qualities of the product.

Try it with some friends – or even home alone, just the two of you. We think it is eminently worth a try.

A Final PS – from both Phoebe and Joe

WE hope that you have enjoyed all, or most, of this book.
We have enjoyed working on it, and writing it, over a two year period.

What we have enjoyed most of all is our conversations and correspondence with all those retired husbands and wives who have been kind enough to open their hearts to us, tell us their problems, and the solutions they have developed to make their marriages Round the Clock happier, more interesting, more satisfying.

We thank them, and we thank you, for your interest in the subject of retirement marriages.

If you have thoughts or ideas or observations on marriage after retirement, we would be delighted to hear from you. We have no idea whether we would be able to answer, or even acknowledge, your letters – but we can assure you we will read them and study them.

So we say 'FAREWELL', and with it our warmest wishes for you and your spouse.

Phoebe Hichens
Joe Wilkerson
c/o Quiller Press Ltd
46 Lillie Road
London SW6 1TN